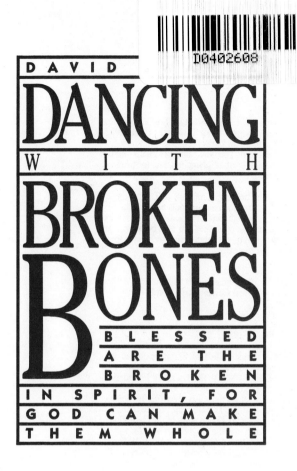

DAVID

DANCING

W   I   T   H

BROKEN
BONES

BLESSED
ARE THE
BROKEN
IN SPIRIT, FOR
GOD CAN MAKE
THEM WHOLE

NAVPRESS ●®
A MINISTRY OF THE NAVIGATORS
P.O. BOX 6000, COLORADO SPRINGS, COLORADO 80934

The Navigators is an international Christian organization. Jesus Christ gave His followers the Great Commission to go and make disciples (Matthew 28:19). The aim of The Navigators is to help fulfill that commission by multiplying laborers for Christ in every nation.

NavPress is the publishing ministry of The Navigators. NavPress publications are tools to help Christians grow. Although publications alone cannot make disciples or change lives, they can help believers learn biblical discipleship, and apply what they learn to their lives and ministries.

© 1987 by David Swartz
All rights reserved, including translation
Library of Congress Catalog Card Number:
  87-62853
ISBN 08910-91483

Second printing, 1988

Unless otherwise identified, all Scripture quotations in this publication are from the *New American Standard Bible* (NASB), © The Lockman Foundation, 1960, 1962, 1963, 1968, 1971, 1972, 1973, 1975, 1977. Other versions used: *The New English Bible* (NEB), © 1961, 1970, The Delegates of the Oxford University Press and The Syndics of the Cambridge University Press; and the *Holy Bible: New International Version* (NIV). Copyright © 1973, 1978, 1984, International Bible Society. Used by permission of Zondervan Bible Publishers.

Printed in the United States of America

To Gay—

Whose love has been my treasure . . .

whose life has been my shelter . . .

whose voice has been the closest thing to God's

for me this side of Heaven.

Contents

Author

David Swartz is pastor of Dubuque Baptist Church in Dubuque, Iowa. He has had a rich background, serving in college campus ministry, street ministry, church outreach ministry, and pastoral ministry.

He received a B.S. from Clarion State College and a M.R.E. from Southern Baptist Theological Seminary.

Dave and his wife, Gay, have two children, Steve and Karen.

Introduction

Our society is caught in a time warp. Time rushes by, bringing changes that both tease and tire us. Technology never gets short of breath trying to make things easier and more convenient, and our appetite for the toys it produces never seems to be satisfied. The technological maze is all around us. Home computers and gourmet food are now common, and fast foods have become even faster.

But in our rush to improve and speed things up, we begin to tire, to sense that we're losing something. A certain quality of life, of relationships, has eluded us. We find ourselves looking over our shoulder to try to recapture them.

Many people want to restore at least the appearance of a simpler lifestyle. It's very fashionable these days to read *The Mother Earth News* or to buy jeans and boots from L. L. Bean. Wood stoves and log houses sell well among the more rustic yuppies. Now everyone from the marinas of Newport Beach to the high-rises of midtown Manhattan can get "back to nature."

While the values of an earlier, simpler era may appeal to some of us, the slower pace of living that undergirded those values does not. Fast-frame living desires the best without waiting. The tension between the desire for quality in life and the desire to have it quickly and at little cost looms within most of us. A recent cartoon says it well. In it, a woman asks a department store salesman if they have a wood-burning microwave oven!

The church is caught in the same tension: the desire for immediate quality at minimal cost. In contrast, some loud voices among us say that we're in the middle of a great revival. At any rate, we're sure more visible. Evangelicals and born-agains of various stripes saturate the air waves, while the Christian book and music markets are booming.

Now Christians drop names as readily as anyone else. We throw out the names of speakers, authors, and artists as if they were old friends, and sit in judgment on what they say as if they were old enemies. The books and tapes we use, together with all the conferences we attend, show our lust for the shortcut. We get home from a weekend retreat with good intentions and a fistful of materials in a three-ring binder that ends up gathering dust on a shelf. Multicolored brochures that boldly advertise "four steps to overcome this" or "ten ways to achieve that" flirt with us in the mail. But while we've become experts on method, we still remain paupers in practice.

Too much of our name-dropping and conference-going is sugarcoating, a veneer of respectability, an evangelical fig leaf we wear in our attempt to cover our barren, superficial lives. In spite of our blatant visibility, society is learning to ignore us, and so we're increasingly talking only to ourselves. This is *not* spiritual awakening! Both the Bible and history describe revival in terms of personal cost and public impact. But why *isn't* it happening? What keeps us from being the Christians we dream of being, so that every brochure and book catalog is nothing more than a tantalizing tease about something we fear we'll never become?

One answer lies in the nature of the spiritual life. Something about a deeper life in Christ at the same time both draws and repels us. We're drawn because of a strong sense of "oughtness," and yet of privilege, too—something that seems as if it was always meant to be and yet is far beyond anything we could ever deserve.

If we truly recognize this privilege, then why should the prospect of knowing Christ repel us? It's simple. The light that shines on Him also glares down on the shabbiness of our lives. Even though this shabbiness threatens to strangle us from within, we've foolishly grown to cherish much of it. Becoming untangled from it may hurt.

And so, relentlessly drawn to the riches in Christ but fearing the light of discovery on our soul, we grope for shortcuts and techniques. Examining the externals rather than our own heart is indeed less painful, but also less illuminating. In the end, too many of us stack our hopes on Band-Aid solutions to problems of the magnitude of spiritual cancer. To keep what we should throw away, although it is comfortably killing us, and to do so at the expense of all Christ wants us to be, is a blind man's bargain.

Many voices call out with so-called answers, but they don't help us decide because they only tell a slender part of the truth. At any carnival, you'll find a row of small booths lit with strings of glaring multicolored lights. A "hawker" stands in front of each booth yelling and pleading, trying to catch the eye of passersby. "It's easy!" they cry. "Just swing a hammer, toss a dart, shoot a basket, or throw a ball, and you, too, can have the prize of your own choice."

The hawkers of the Christian midway are often strong on words like "love," "joy," "peace," "acceptance," and so on. While all these words have solid biblical roots, these spiritual salesmen usually neglect another word that highlights another dimension of spiritual truth. That word is "holiness." It's a sobering word, especially to those of us who have exchanged solemn intimacy, genuine personal knowledge of God, for mere familiarity and gushiness in our relationship with Him.

Knowing God instead of knowing about Him means baring our soul in the light of His holiness. There's no avoiding it for those who want to go deeper with God. It's not easy. It means looking at our sin and calling it just that, without flinching, even though our shame screams out for us to turn away. It means that words like "Incarnation" and "atonement" aren't just academic toys for theologians to toss around, but that they are poignant passwords that tell what happened when, in the historic backwaters of the Roman Empire, theology got dirty, paying a horrible price in order to free men from their aeons of sin.

But standing our ground here when everything in us wants to run away is important. The path to growth and fruitfulness in the Christian life leads through a door marked *brokenness*. Brokenness is the trophy for those wanting to know God's presence so very much that they are willing to endure the heat of His holiness. Although it may not feel like it at the time, those people who embrace brokenness—what Jesus referred to as poverty and humility of spirit within those who recognize their need for God (Matthew 5:3-5)—instead of running away into closets of pity and bitterness are penetrating through to possibilities of significant growth and service.

A wise person learns from the failures and mistakes of others. We should take note, for the Bible strips away the superficial masks of religion and shows us the complex, struggling lives of people just like us. The following pages will take us through the heart and soul of one of those lives. King David knew the utter blackness of sin. But since we, too, know that bane of spiritual darkness, no finger pointing is allowed. David's life was bared not just before God but before men. We need compassion.

Finally, David will show us as individuals and as a church that the road to joy, peace, and power isn't a high and easy road at all, but a low, less-traveled path. Not many sermon nibblers or cassette tasters find it. Only broken sinners know the path.

I know the way very well. While I may not have an advanced degree, I'm shamefully experienced. But God has cultivated the mire of my past into a garden where His grace is turning the pain, sweat, mistakes, and guilt into something genuinely solid and good. The more I see of it, the more I feel so undeserving of what He does—and yet I press forward like a kid at a toy store window to see what He will do next.

If you've read even this far, you, too, are probably hungering for more from God than you are experiencing right now. Christ died for that part that is missing in my life and your life. And, despite its mocking and ridicule, a lost world watches us closely because its surplus of technological trinkets just doesn't satisfy.

David is now about to teach us a song—Psalm 51—that isn't easy to sing. But we must try. For after we truly learn it, the fullest music of heaven will never be more than a prayer away.

CHAPTER ONE

You Can't Run Away

*Be gracious to me, O God, according
to Thy lovingkindness;
According to the greatness of Thy
compassion blot out my transgressions.*

*Wash me thoroughly from my iniquity,
And cleanse me from my sin.
Psalm 51:1-2*

There are few snobs among drowning men. Gasping and spluttering, they will seize anything, no matter how small, attempting to hold themselves afloat. But picture this: rescuers throw a life jacket to a man in deep water, who is struggling on the brink of exhaustion. However, rather than just slipping it on and thereby saving his life, he rolls the jacket between his numb fingers and flings it away in disgust. Gurgling beneath the waves for the last time he says, "That's really not my style. Have you got something in a tweed with a belt in the back?" Of course, no one facing death would be so foolish.

There may not be many snobs among drowning men, but many play with spiritual truth as if it were a toy. Many people who have been offered a door to life in Christ hesitate because some aspect of the gospel doesn't suit their taste. The Cross of Jesus Christ causes us to back off for any number of reasons. Granted, Jesus was a moral man and a great teacher. But the only way to

God? Are we really all sinners? A recent cartoon portrays a well-heeled woman with her pastor. She says, "Quite frankly, repentance isn't my strong suit. How about if I just let you use my beach house for two months a year and call it even?"

Confronted with God's remedy for our fatal condition, we race in the opposite direction, looking for substitutes and excuses. Some turn to reincarnation, yoga, or even yogurt. We can expect this of those who are spiritually blind and lost (Romans 1:21-32, 1 Corinthians 2:11-14). But what about the sad phenomenon of people within the church who wholeheartedly agree that Christ was good enough to save them yet selectively refuse to serve Him beyond the limits of personal comfort and convenience?

We've all been bitten

It's so easy to shoot at others. But I must admit that I, too, am sometimes guilty of certain symptoms of the "kneeling Pharisee syndrome." This includes a slight squint of the eyes and drawing up a corner of the mouth to one notch above a smirk. A voice keeps whispering in the heart, "I'm glad I'm not like them!" But the story of David jars us back to our senses with a shocking slap. Sin doesn't just lie at the other guy's doorstep. It bites us all. The sordid details behind Psalm 51 are well-known.

In an unguarded moment, King David yielded to his lust, having an affair with Bathsheba, the wife of one of his most faithful soldiers. When he discovered that Bathsheba was pregnant, David constructed a network of lies to deceive her husband, Uriah. As a last desperate resort, David arranged circumstances to ensure Uriah's death.

But before the head wagging starts among those who would sit in judgment over David, something else needs to be remembered, something that should leave any smirks limp on our lips. David was a man after God's own heart. He was no spiritual wimp. But then shouldn't he have known better? In fact, he *did* know better. And yet that knowledge didn't stop him.

We often know better as well, but it doesn't always stop us. The pull of our "wants" often prevails. What about a willful, deliberate sin, a sin that takes one look at the Cross and says, "I know You did all that for me, but I want to indulge my desires in this area just this one time; it's a perfect opportunity; and . . . I just want to"?

We can't deny that it happens. An honest look at ourselves won't allow it. But what can we do about it? We can start where David did: with a cry from our spiritual innards for *mercy*.

David was a man who needed no one's permission for his actions. He was the king. He could get anything he wanted. In the eyes of men, David stood at the pinnacle of his world. But his standing in the eyes of God was not as secure. Any power David had before men was useless before God.

David had to go through a process of being confronted by God, to be called on the spiritual carpet. He anguished over his own betrayal of his Master's trust. He pleaded with God to be tenderly affected toward him by showing undeserved pity. This was no brash demand, but a prayer desperately sweated out on tiptoe. It was the screaming of a man's spirit who did not want God to deal with him on the basis of what he deserved but on the basis of the mercy God had shown him in the past.

Nothing cuts more sharply across the grain of our thinking. We live in times when people are intent on getting whatever they can because of their "rights." Commercials croon, "You can have it all." Not only can we have it, but somehow we think we actually deserve it. Pleading for undeserved pity is thus rather alien to our world.

A poisonous trio

In David's heart there lurked a darkness—a deliberate, stiffnecked refusal to submit to rightful authority. Here was a king who expected complete submission from his subjects, yet couldn't live up to the standard he demanded of others. That's why eventually he asked God to "blot out [his] transgressions" (Psalm 51:1). David's basic *transgression* was taking a deliberate step over the line challenging God's right to be God. Paul described us all when he said, "Even though they knew God, they did not honor Him as God" (Romans 1:21).

And why don't we honor God? Because we are too busy honoring ourselves. This is no accident. It's intentional and often premeditated. The concept of transgression confronts our smug notions of maturity and sophistication with the truth that, underlying it all, there is a robust selfishness that refuses to worship anything but the person in the mirror. We should know this selfishness well, because it is a major driving force behind us all.

David also admitted that he experienced "iniquity" within himself (Psalm 51:2). The idea here is one of being warped or twisted. One day a bunch of us were working on a house. Sawing through some red oak, we wondered why the saw overheated and jammed. A quick look at the plank showed a warp running the length of the board. Although it looked fine, for our purposes it was useless. Until we looked again carefully, we were unable to notice how out-of-line this board really was.

Iniquity is the warped, pulsating, driving hunger of desire that makes us go blind to what is right as we go grasping for what we want. Wrong seems not only right, but desirable. Real iniquity is when the rationalizations are delivered with a practiced agility. It's when a man can gaze on the wife of another, lust for her, sleep with her, and then murder her husband in an attempt to conceal an out-of-wedlock pregnancy. Knowing what's wrong doesn't always stop us. In fact, sometimes it only makes our mouth water. That's moral twistedness—*iniquity.*

Lastly, David recognized "sin" within himself. *Sin* means to fall short of God's standard. David had fallen short of very little in his life. Politically, militarily, socially, and economically, he achieved virtually all that was possible for a man of his time. But that was the problem. Comparing ourselves with others is easy. In attempting to justify our direction in life and to build some foundation for self-worth, it's not difficult to find a way to tear down someone who in some way makes us uncomfortable and envious. In the process, we refine both gossip and destructive criticism to a level approaching that of spiritual gifts.

But what do we do when the massive achievements of our earthly lives stand alongside God's yardstick and register as a pile of filthy rags? What do we do when we discover that God is not a respecter of persons, résumés, Phi Beta Kappa keys, portfolios of blue chip stocks and securities, or even how many points we can score on an arcade video game? No matter how fiercely we strive for success and try to always display ourselves in the best light, our best efforts fall short. They miss the mark. They fall short of what God both expects and requires.

This is the picture of sin described in Romans 3:23: "All have sinned and fall short of the glory of God." That poisonous trio of transgressions, iniquities, and sins infiltrates our fallen species. For David to see himself in this way was devastating. And it should be for us, too. But there seems to be a certain sanity that rises out of even the most scarring things souls can endure. This knowledge hurt David deeply, *but* it was the first step toward putting things right.

I once served briefly as a hospital chaplain. As part of my duties, I led services at a local mental health clinic. The first time I entered that building, I had many fears that weren't in any way relieved by all those electrically locked doors I had to pass through. But after being with these people for only a few minutes, something strange happened. All my fears were gone. I began wondering why all these people were there. They seemed like some of the sanest people I'd ever met. They simply seemed to be saying, "We can't run anymore."

That's David. And it's us, too. It took the prophetic impact of Nathan's accusation to bring David to his senses. Only then could he see that his situation required some desperate measures. He longed to see the deep stain of his transgression blotted out, as when an ink stain is totally soaked up. He yearned for his iniquity to be washed away, as when clothes are beaten on a rock or in a washing trough. And he dreamed of the day when his sin would be cleansed, and his soul would appear bright and shining as if there had never been a stain.

We misread both the text and David's heart if we think of these as casual requests. The nerve ends of the man's soul are laid bare and throbbing. Suddenly he realizes that he can't run anymore. He can't offer excuses. He recognizes that it's time to hold his peace. D. Martyn Lloyd-Jones made this very point in his treatment of Romans 3:19-20:

> How do you know whether a man is a Christian? The answer is that his mouth is shut. I like this forthrightness of the Gospel. People need to have their mouths shut, "stopped." They are forever talking about God, and criticizing God, and pontificating about what God should or should not do, and asking, "Why does God allow this or that?" You do not begin to be a Christian until your mouth is shut, is stopped, and you are speechless and have nothing to say.[1]

David's mouth is shut. This psalm is sung through clenched teeth and pursed lips. Some of us know well this kind of humble silence, while others need to make its acquaintance. Sin, iniquity, and transgression are not some other guy's problem, nor are they something we left behind after we became Christians. Regardless of appearances, we eventually come to know the bitter, convicting, ego-shattering truth in our hearts.

Or do we? Many people around us desire a spiritual awakening for Christ's church. "Just how will we know when it comes?" they ask. Many are looking primarily for tangible results. Increases in church membership and in financial giving, along with the strong emotional surges that often accompany the moving of God's Spirit—that's what we want.

But a study of spiritual awakenings reveals something deeper, more foundational. Both Scripture and history show that a sharp inner conviction of sin leading to changed lives is usually the necessary cutting edge for genuine spiritual awakening. Note Peter's words on Pentecost: "Let all the house of Israel know for certain that God has made Him both Lord and Christ—this Jesus whom you crucified" (Acts 2:36).

When God's Word is broken open, it should provide meat for the soul, not just chewing gum for the mind. Peter didn't offer warm fuzzies, promise material prosperity, or give an affirming word. He simply told them the truth. He told the bewildered Jews the truth about God the Father, the truth about His Son, and the truth about themselves. It cut deeply.

Like the wicked queen in *Snow White,* we've grown to love the narcissistic mirrors in our hearts that tell us, "You're the fairest of them all." But truth is an iconoclast that delights in smashing those mirrors. It is a persistent nag that refuses to go away just because its revealing message may be socially unpopular and morally inconvenient.

From David's lips, the truth finds us defiantly rebellious, morally and spiritually twisted, falling short of both God's standards and our own. That's us—you and me. But there's hope. The first step in the healing of a problem is admitting our need. A man or woman who confesses no curse certainly feels no need of a cure. A remedy, one older than time itself with its genesis in the mind of the Creator of the universe, is ready at hand. But first we must sing a bitter song along with David. We must soberly admit that, left to ourselves, our souls are terminally ill.

We must not deceive ourselves. There aren't a vast number of gods to choose from. Our options are narrowed down to one: a holy God who confronts our evasive patterns at every turn. We must face Him! There is nowhere to hide, nowhere to run away.

For He pursues us, He finds us everywhere. But He chases us in order to save, not to judge; to help, not to destroy. The deep inner healing we all need can come from no other source. It must come from Him alone.

NOTES:
1. David Martyn Lloyd-Jones, *Atonement and Justification, Romans 3:25-4:25* (Grand Rapids: Zondervan, 1970), page 19.

CHAPTER TWO

Taking Stock of the Darkness Within

For I know my transgressions,
And my sin is ever before me.

Against Thee, Thee only, I have sinned,
And done what is evil in Thy sight,
So that Thou art justified when Thou dost speak,
And blameless when Thou dost judge.
Psalm 51:3-4

■

One day we took the kids to a children's zoo. Most of these places have the same kinds of animals: deer, goats, and ducks for kids to chase, feed, and pet. But this one was different. There were armadillos and tarantulas!

I was captivated by a display in the middle of the floor where what appeared to be a stuffed boa constrictor was draped over a makeshift tree. I took the opportunity to examine him from head to tail. At one point only two inches separated our noses. Then his head moved. So did I. I'd underestimated the ominous reality and danger of my friend in the tree.

It's easy to do the same in our spiritual lives. Most sin appears to be pretty mundane stuff, and yet it is quite lethal. We ensure our own spiritual undoing whenever we underestimate the strength of our opponent. We go around giving lip service to "crucifying the flesh with its lusts," and then we move callously and carelessly on our way. But an enemy neglected or taken for granted still has life

23

and bite, like my very much alive friend at the zoo.

When our lives get flabby, we get careless and soon forget the lethal nature of the sins that surround us. It's not enough to merely stop running away from God. We must pause to take stock of the darkness we have allowed to enter within us. God wants to show us all the dark places, to shine His penetrating light of truth into our innermost being. Even though our sin may seem rather familiar, harmless, and almost boring to us after living with it for so long, God wants us to recognize that it is nothing less than spiritual poison. To Him, sin is neither familiar, comfortable, boring, nor harmless. It is a venom that attacks the spiritual health and vitality of all His beloved children.

Only those who are in Christ know the real strength of sin and temptation. Realizing the true strength of any force comes only with resistance. Those who worship themselves are merely flowing along with the current. They have no idea of sin's deadly potency. A person outside of Christ experiences sin in the same way that a fish understands wetness. They're both unaware, since each lives in his respective condition constantly. Each knows no other level of existence.

But although fish may not be consciously aware of wetness, the Holy Spirit relentlessly makes men aware of sin. He inventories and prods the darkest corners of our lives, where we've accumulated various collections of spiritual death for years. And, much to our horror and chagrin, He forthrightly announces to us what He's found. At that point, we are compelled to listen. Wisely, David did so.

Who, me?

The darkness in David's heart had at least three aspects. First, he couldn't claim ignorance. He couldn't innocently ask, "Who, me?" He knew. David laments, "I know my transgressions, and my sin is ever before me."

As both a Christian and a pastor, I've found myself in

discussions (and arguments) on Scripture and other related sub-jects. One of my greatest frustrations used to be my inability to prove to people the reality of their sin. My sharpest arguments would fall flat. Looking back, all I was really trying to do was dazzle my opponents with some fancy theological footwork. Now, when I talk about Christ, I still mention sin, but I rarely launch into long philosophical arguments. That's because I've learned two things.

One is that I'm not the Holy Spirit. Much of my wrangling was a weak attempt to do on my own what only the Spirit can do. Also, I've learned that in theological argument or debate, truth often becomes a secondary concern. Admitting that the other person is right about my being a sinner just isn't the same as admitting that I'm wrong about who led the National League in batting in 1950. Our egos will seldom let us lose. Somewhere along the way, coming out on top becomes more important than learning the truth.

Now in dealing with people, I assume three things about everyone I meet. First of all, this person's sin isn't an illusion. It's real. Second, it's a reality that the Holy Spirit is often confronting, whether I can see it or not. And third, this person usually feels the awful weight of the sin's reality, regardless of what he will admit to me or even to himself. I no longer have to win.

The hills of North Carolina hold some of the most beautiful vistas of countryside to be found anywhere. The view stretching out over my in-laws' farm seems so calm and serene. And then you see them. Swirling in lazy circles in the distance, buzzards hover and slowly descend. The initial serenity is suddenly fouled by the new knowledge that, in spite of appearances, there is something dead out there.

At the end of a fairly good day, when our defenses are relaxing, our sense of sin can rise seemingly out of nowhere, like vultures out of a Carolina sky, and slowly spiral home to roost. All externals notwithstanding, there is something dead in there.

Look at David. Many wouldn't see anything wrong with much that happened. Sure, Bathsheba became pregnant. But he married her, didn't he? True, he did murder the husband, attempting to hide it. But I've met many people who could justify even that in their own minds. They've ruined other lives, some have even killed them, and yet they feel no remorse—only regret at getting caught.

Scripture says, "It is impossible for the blood of bulls and goats to take away sins" (Hebrews 10:4). If the blood of animals won't take away the sins of a man, neither will a wedding ceremony. Picture David lying in bed at night beside slumbering, softly-breathing Bathsheba. If things were as they should be, the thoughts belonging to a husband in this situation should normally be ones of satisfaction and contentment. But how can these thoughts be David's as he lies there plagued with memories of lust, cowardice, and murder that even a marriage bed can't conceal? Daylight would bring no relief. Seeing her at meals and random glimpses caught of her in the palace throughout the day would only bring sharp stabs from the past. How many conversations could they have that would be outside the shadow of their conscience and memories of what had been done?

One of the most difficult conditions for many people to tolerate is an absence of outside stimuli to occupy and distract them. But this is, ironically enough, a good test for determining how someone is getting along spiritually. Christian men and women throughout the ages have sought out some peaceful place for taking stock of their lives and meditating on God and His Word.

The test is this: can you cope with silence? It sounds so easy, deceptively so. Modern man feels that he has to surround himself with constant background noise and other sensory distractions. Why? Because he cannot stand being truly alone with himself for very long. Visit a college dormitory and note the stereos blasting in almost every room. When you walk into a motel room or into your home after being out, how long is it before someone turns on the television, even if no one watches it? It's not necessarily human beings that we have to have around us. We've devised any number of electronic substitutes to keep us from being alone.

But what's so bad about being alone, anyhow? Nothing in and of itself. As a matter of fact, it's a very healthy thing to be by oneself occasionally. Meditation, which has been given a bad image because of its association with Eastern religions and cults, can become a fundamental building block of deep character when it takes place in the context of Scripture and a setting of silence. George Herbert said, "By all means take some time to be alone and see what your soul doth wear." Maybe that's precisely why so many people avoid being alone in silence. When you're all alone, your true self rises like flotsam to the surface to face you. And what floats to the surface isn't guaranteed to be pretty. David said, "My sin is ever before me."

Nowhere to hide

A second aspect of David's recognition of the darkness within him lies in the words, "Against Thee, Thee only, I have sinned." A grand old theological concept raises its head here: omnipresence. Simply, it means that God is present in all places at all times. David didn't have the luxury of one device our society now subscribes to in epidemic proportions. He could not escape.

Escape has become a fashionable alternative in almost any situation. If the urban-suburban rat race and the mortgage become a strain, just chuck it all for the backwoods of Idaho or Maine. If you're unappreciated on the job or can't advance as fast as you'd like, just bolt to a rival firm. Maybe your marriage is beset with "irreconcilable differences." Or perhaps you've decided that your spouse needs his or her "freedom." No matter what desire for escape is taking place in our lives, it invariably indicates either that we're unwilling to change or that our selfish desires are being restricted, much to our resentment.

But God is one person we just can't escape from. Scripture describes God as being present everywhere at all times.

> Where can I go from Thy Spirit?
> Or where can I flee from Thy presence?
> If I ascend to heaven, Thou art there;
> If I make my bed in Sheol, behold, Thou art there.
> If I take the wings of the dawn,
> If I dwell in the remotest part of the sea,
> Even there Thy hand will lead me,
> And Thy right hand will lay hold of me. (Psalm 139:7-10)

Have you ever had to endure the presence of someone you had deeply offended—a family member, a friend, or someone at work? David had sinned against *God,* and there was no way of escaping it.

The power of human choice

A third aspect of David's dark situation can be encapsulated in another theological word: omniscience. In short, God knows everything. He sees and knows it all—even the bad things.

Something must be said here on David's behalf. Once he had been confronted, he made no excuses. Moral nakedness shows how our inner character can stand up when our last flimsy excuse, like a fig leaf, flutters to the ground. It's one thing to know that God knows about our sin, but quite another to agree with God's estimate of what He's seen.

David admitted doing evil in God's sight. His honesty is rare and refreshing. Never did he resort to the God-needs-more-information syndrome, which says, "Okay, I knew it was wrong, but if all the facts were known. . . ." But David knew that all the facts *were* known. God is both omniscient and omnipresent. He is an eyewitness of both the deed and the heart. There is nothing, no new information, that can sway His opinion of our actions. God is always proved right when He speaks and always justified when He judges. He lacks neither information nor insight.

This raises an important point. If God knows all about my sin, then why do I need to confess it? First of all, Scripture links the forgiveness of sin with its confession (1 John 1:9). The goal of confessing sin is not the sharing of information but the restoration of the relationship between myself and God.

Keith Miller provides a graphic illustration. Imagine you're called out of town for a few days on business. Finishing early, you arrive home a couple of days ahead of schedule and walk in unannounced. Hearing a sound from the bedroom, you walk to that part of the house and stand outside the closed door in shocked amazement. Your spouse is having an affair. Stunned, you leave without making your presence known.

Later you return and both of you act as if nothing has happened. But that's not so. Your mate has violated the intimacy of your relationship, and both of you know it. But even though both of you know it, there is little hope that the relationship will be restored until what you both know gets into the open and forgiveness is granted.

It boils down to a single question: What do you really want? The power of human choice is frightening. Decisions that many people make so glibly will have an impact and implications far into our future years and beyond. The twin realities of heaven and hell are sobering reminders that God, in judging mankind, will simply be giving people what they chose.

Again, what do we really want? Are we desperate to appear right both in our eyes and in the eyes of others? If so, we have our reward right now, but we also have an appointment with an all-seeing, all-knowing God that we will certainly keep.

Confession means confronting ourselves
Scripture describes salvation from many angles. What God has done for men through Jesus Christ is like a diamond spinning in a

brilliant light. With the slightest turn, the light is refracted at different angles, revealing shades and colors we could not have anticipated till then.

Too many of us, however, settle for mere religion as a substitute for what God intended: a beautiful, multifaceted relationship. Between our boards, councils, committees, and other meetings with neither purpose nor end, we swallow enough religious formality to gag a Pharisee. Caught in a whirlwind of potluck suppers, we show ourselves weak where David was strong. We're often too busy doing fairly good things for God to give attention to the very best things that can build a deep, continuous walk with Him. Most of our Christian life becomes consumed with "things," and in the process we lose track of the most important part of all: Christ Himself. And so our confessions, too, are often superficial and self-centered.

One day my son was caught red-handed in deliberate disobedience. I could just see the wheels of his mind spinning, thinking, "Okay, how can I get out of this?" That's the attitude of too many. Okay, I've sinned. Now, how can I get off the hook? Such a mind-set is way off track.

My own view of this situation was quite different. My relationship with my son had been breached, at least temporarily, by his disobedience. Things just couldn't go on normally until the issue had been dealt with, resolved, and the relationship properly restored.

That's God's perspective. God is described as being holy. His nature is of such moral purity and perfection that people find it both terrifying and alluring. From God's vantage point, sin cannot be swept away under the guise of His love for us. Much in our day that falls into the category of God's "love" or our "love" for each other is simply moral cowardice. It's an excuse for sin. God wants a relationship with us that has been honestly resolved and properly restored. God Himself took the initiative and paid the terrible, ultimate cost in terms of the Cross of Christ. "God demonstrated

His own love toward us, in that while we were yet sinners, Christ died for us" (Romans 5:8).

Too many people who cling to the name of Jesus Christ merely want off the hook—a cheap confession followed by a speedy absolution, amounting to spiritual license to go back and live their lives as if Christ had never died. But in our desire to escape, we forfeit the most precious privilege granted to us: knowing God. We must understand exactly what we risk throwing away.

Jesus said, "No one knows who the Son is except the Father, and who the Father is except the Son, and anyone to whom the Son wills to reveal Him" (Luke 10:22). I remember my father very well. He was a steelworker, a crane operator in the assembly yard of a U.S. Steel plant outside of Pittsburgh. The men he worked with knew him, too. Some feared him; all respected him. More than one man owed his life to "Bub" Swartz. He told supervisors and foremen what to do, and they did it! Dad said to me once, "David, when I throw the lever and lift twenty-five tons of steel into the air, I outrank the president of U.S. Steel." That wasn't bragging; he was telling the truth.

But all those welders, riveters, set-up men, and hook-up men who worked with him never knew him like I did. They saw him as a tough man who had to be respected, someone they would have no trouble with as long as they did their job. I saw him in ways they never would have imagined.

Dad was a man who gave me two incredible gifts. One was the gift of touch. Right up through the day I left home to be married, I knew his touch of affection in a variety of ways: a hug, a swat on the backside, an arm around my shoulder, a tousling of my hair. His hands were huge, but always tender.

Dad also gave me the gift of tears. The men at the mill thought my dad was tough. They wouldn't have recognized the man who sat and wept with me when my dog died, and who allowed me to cry with him when his dad died.

On the day of my wedding, both of Dad's gifts were intertwined. All through the ceremony, the two of us wept for joy. Regardless of what others thought, neither of us was embarrassed, because the tears were something shared between us.

Later that day, my bride and I went to the motel to change clothes. Dad and I hadn't had much opportunity to talk after the ceremony, so when he walked into the room, the response was spontaneous. A twenty-three-year-old man ran across the room and leaped into the air. Dad caught me and held me up off the floor in a long hug. I can still feel the warmth of his body and the gentle strength of his arms. I can still smell his Old Spice and the minty aroma of the Tums he always carried. For all the time they spent with him, those steelworkers didn't know half the man that was there.

While people believe all kinds of things about God, think how much better Jesus knows Him, how much better the Son knows the Father. To even imagine the intimacies that pass between Them seems instantly a terrible, even sacrilegious, invasion of privacy. But it needn't be. Jesus is willing to share that family relationship with us so that we can know the same kind of intimacy for ourselves. However, such deep personal treasures are not for just anyone. After the verse just quoted, Jesus went on to say to His disciples, "Blessed are the eyes which see the things you see, for I say to you, that many prophets and kings wished to see the things which you see, and did not see them, and to hear the things which you hear, and did not hear them" (Luke 10:23-24).

Do we really want to throw this kind of treasure away? Look at what your soul is wearing. Be alone with your heart, even the blackest chambers. Take stock of the darkness within. And then ask for light. Even though you wince in its brilliance, call everything you find there with the name God has for it. This process may hurt. It almost always does. But don't most forms of healing involve pain? Taking an honest look at your inner darkness might be agonizing in the short run, but it's a step in the right direction in the long run. Yours is the race of a long-distance runner.

CHAPTER THREE

The Deep Roots of Darkness

Behold, I was brought forth in iniquity,
And in sin my mother conceived me.
Psalm 51:5

■

As I write, a yawning pit in the earth stands between our home and the church. In the near future some much-needed classrooms will fill that hole. While some people have made the inevitable comments about progress, sometimes I'm not so sure. An old friend bit the dust in the process.

A massive oak tree almost a hundred years old had to come down to make way for concrete and steel. Whether blazing red and orange in an autumn sunset or standing barren and black against a cloudless winter sky, the two of us had shared some good times on the hill.

It died hard. The giant that stood towering above the earth gave way quickly to the chainsaw. But the oak saved its real muscle for the bulldozer that was sent to plow out the stump. They sat in the pit, glowering at each other like a couple of surly old bulldogs. Then the bulldozer lowered its blade and chugged forward. Wham! The stump didn't even budge—not one inch.

Time and again the bulldozer came with greater speed and from greater distances, but the stump held its ground.

Getting nowhere fast, the construction people withdrew their defeated bulldozer and returned with a large backhoe. It wasn't until they had done some extensive chopping at the roots that the stump tottered and finally fell. Then we learned by observation that the root system of that old oak had been as massive under the ground as the limbs of the tree had been above it.

Stained to the core

When we try to plow stumps of sin from our lives, we find that they don't give way easily. That's because the roots run deep. Just as great wisdom can uproot and reveal the folly of great ignorance, great light alone is able to reveal great darkness.

David had made the sobering discovery that the problem lay much deeper than he'd realized. The root system that fed the stump of his sin was as extensive as the mighty branches that once lifted toward the sky. In the beginning of Psalm 51, David started unraveling some painful truths. But now, in verse 5, he had to acknowledge that the problem ran far deeper than his sinful actions; it ran to his very nature. "Behold I was brought forth in iniquity, and in sin my mother conceived me."

Before dismissing this verse as being off the deep end, take a second look at who's speaking. This wasn't the moping reaction of a low-esteemed person who delighted in flogging himself. This was King David, the ruler of Israel, which was the nation of God. Even in the early days before the anointing from Samuel, he showed strong signs of leadership and deep integrity. He stood as one of very few whose greatness was realized in his lifetime. David wasn't a man who spent a lot of energy running himself down. His normal response to his actions right now would have been concealment, not negative self-reflection. But another line of thought was forced upon him. It was the giant of *truth* David now had to face.

The bitter essence of David's self-exposure is this: *Surely I have been a sinner from birth.* Nathan's accusation had sliced through David's heart like a sword blade. It's a humbling moment when God penetrates your heart, revealing what is really there. David goes on to say that he'd been sinful from the time his mother had conceived him. This has nothing to do with human sexuality itself being sinful. David is saying, "I am really this way at the core of my being and there has never been a time when I wasn't this way." This couldn't have been just a ho-hum admission of fact. He must have shaken his head in horror and loathing at the thought.

Theologians have left us a word describing this condition: *depravity.* It's a word that raises both questions (because we don't understand it) and blood pressures (because, uncomfortably, some of us *do* understand it all too well). It doesn't mean that all people are as actively wicked as they could be. As I observe both the daily newspaper and the daily sinfulness of my own heart, I'm reminded that people are constantly devising new ways of defying God. Neither does it mean that sinful people are incapable of noble thoughts or good actions.

Actually, the word "depravity" has a twofold meaning.[1] First of all, nothing in man can commend him to a holy God. This cuts painfully across the deeply ingrained notion that we can somehow ensure our acceptance by God through the good things we do. Here is where that sweet little old lady fails the test. She's always been little. But she hasn't always been old, and, if you knew her as God does, she hasn't always been sweet, either!

Second, depravity means that this inborn corruption extends to every part of man's nature, including all his faculties. In a nutshell, we're *tainted.* To me, tainted used to mean the beginning stages of decay. But one day my thinking changed.

My brother-in-law is a trapper. His knowledge of animals and their life patterns is extensive. I was watching him one day as he was cutting up the meat of a wildcat he had shot. He was going to use it for fox bait. The meat was sealed in a quart jar, and then the jar was left in the sun for three days. When Ronnie took the lid off that jar, the word "tainted" took on new shades of meaning. David was talking about a condition much more serious than a mere slip or an occasional mistake.

In an age of spiritual flabbiness, this view of man's corrupt nature smacks of fanaticism. But even a brief glimpse into lives of dedicated believers reveals a deep awareness of sin and unworthiness. Consider the great apostle Paul, who said:

Christ Jesus came into the world to save sinners, among whom I am foremost of all. (1 Timothy 1:15)

Or Saint Francis of Assisi:

Great and glorious God and Thou, Lord Jesus, I pray Ye shed abroad Your light in the darkness of my mind.[2]

Or John Calvin:

Whenever I descended into myself, or raised my mind to Thee, extreme terror seized me—terror which no expiations nor satisfaction could cure. And the more closely I examined myself, the sharper the stings with which my conscience was pricked.[3]

Or George Whitefield:

The blessed Spirit was all this time purifying my soul. All my former gross and notorious, and even my heart sins, also, were now set home upon me.[4]

The same is true of all those anonymous people who have come to Christ but not to the spotlight. Humility and awareness of sin are not the exclusive property of people with a "special" call.

The outlook of our little world was black and one night we agreed that we were two evil spirits on account of our gross unfaithfulness to the Crucified, and we almost resolved to flee from the presence of the Lord to some Tarshish because our hearts were so black.[5]

The God who pulls us from the pit

Before the excuses and rationalizations begin, read David's words again carefully. This isn't the raving of a guilt-ridden man, but the verdict of the Word of God. Do we accept this estimate that we are born in sin? For many evangelicals, the *atonement* (Christ's payment for man's sin, thus reconciling God and man) has become merely an intellectual exercise. While Paul claimed that we should put no confidence in works of the flesh (Philippians 3:3), that seems to be exactly where the confidence of many a church lies. The powerlessness of the church within society, in spite of our size and visibility, betrays that we don't have a very deep sense of having been forgiven. Our sense of sin is shallow, to put it mildly.

In too many of our churches, conversations on spiritual things seem out of place. We're content to measure our progress in terms of big buildings, big budgets, big giving, big youth groups, big Sunday school attendance. We tend to think more in terms of quantity rather than quality. As long as it's big—even if the fruit of the Spirit isn't visible—God must be pleased. But in our obsession with quantity, is it possible that we're failing to build our foundation with quality?

The size of a church, an organization, or a group never absolves the individual of responsibility. An educator in close contact with churches and leaders, Howard Hendricks, said, "I have been in the ministry just long enough to be totally unimpressed with the visible success of men. I have learned that it is possible to be eminently and visibly successful in the eyes of men but at the same time a total failure in the eyes of God."[6] Does belonging to the biggest church in town, where the pastor is on television and has written books, mean that we don't need to be confronted with what we are in light of the holiness of God? Does having the biggest Sunday school attendance in the state mean that we are entitled to ignore our sinful condition in the sight of our crucified Savior?

By way of contrast, God looked past our externals, regardless of their size and prestige, and what He saw moved Him to desperate but deliberate measures. God came down into our flesh to tear away sin's deep roots, which were wrapped like strangling vines around men's souls. Beyond Jesus, God has nothing greater, nothing more to give. But that is exactly what was, and is, needed. Nothing else could ever suffice.

A few years ago my in-laws were having plumbing problems and had to dig up their septic tank. Since they lived out in the country, they didn't think leaving the tank open would be much of a risk. But a stray dog foraging in the compost heap came down through the yard and fell into the hole. His howls split the night air and brought my young children running to my side, their eyes bugging out in fear.

The next morning I went to find the dog who had sunk in the ooze of the septic tank up to his belly. I had three choices. I could just leave him there—but my soft heart for animals would not allow that. I could put a ladder down into the hole so that the dog could possibly climb out. Or, third, I could go down into the tank and lift him out. The second option fortunately worked, much to my relief!

God faced a similar situation in dealing with man. Man's deepest problem isn't so much related to what he *does,* but with what he *is.* The more we struggle with this spiritual dilemma, the more we find ourselves belly-deep in a sin problem we just can't escape from.

God could not ignore us in this predicament; He loved us too much. And no man-made ladder could reach the bottom, if there ever was one, of the septic tank of our sinful nature. The only alternative God had was to go down into the ooze alongside men in their sin and pull them out. That is exactly what Jesus Christ did.

A deep cleaning is what we all need, but deep cleaning sometimes feels like rough handling. In the fantasy novel *Voyage of the Dawn Treader* by C. S. Lewis, a boy named Eustace enters a cave that contains a dragon's treasure of gold and jewels. After imagining what he will do with all the stolen treasure, he falls asleep, only to awaken and find that he has turned into a dragon himself. At the end of himself, Eustace meets Aslan the lion, who is the Christ figure. Aslan offers to remove the old scaly skin. Eustace agrees. Here he describes what Aslan does to him:

> "The very first tear he made was so deep that I thought it had gone right into my heart. And when he began pulling the skin off, it hurt worse than anything I've ever felt. The only thing that made me able to bear it was just the pleasure of feeling the stuff peel off. . . . Then he caught hold of me—I didn't like that much for I was very tender underneath now that I'd no skin on—and threw me into the water. It smarted like anything, but only for a moment. After that it became perfectly delicious. . . ."[7]

But in showing us what we truly are deep down inside, God's intent isn't to destroy. Actually, He uproots and flattens only so He can rebuild.

> God, the Master Workman, will not break all before Him in a mighty wave of destruction, only to retire once more to His heaven. What God breaks He can also be counted on to remake. . . . Broken men are pliant men. When a person has reached the end of himself he is ready for a new beginning. The broken individual has no inclination or ability to

tell God how to proceed. He is ready for any changes God desires and is now able to regard whatever God does as a source of joy and perpetual thanksgiving.[8]

Now the questions about our own deep roots fall heavy upon us. Do we share the strong desire of David to get to the bottom of our dilemma? Do we want growth in Christ all that badly, or are we giving mere lip service to our faith? Nowhere does God promise us growth without cost. But He does promise that whatever sacrifice we make to become like Christ is well worth the effort.

NOTES:
1. Charles C. Ryrie, "Depravity," *Baker Dictionary of Theology,* E. F. Harrison, ed. (Grand Rapids: Baker Book House, 1960), page 164.
2. James Burns, *Revivals: Their Laws and Leaders* (Grand Rapids: Baker Book House, 1960), page 90.
3. Burns, *Revivals,* page 211.
4. A. Skevington Wood, *The Inextinguishable Blaze: Spiritual Renewal and Advance in the 18th Century* (Grand Rapids: Eerdmans, 1960), page 86.
5. Eifion Evans, *The Welsh Revival of 1904* (Bryntirion, Wales: Evangelical Press of Wales, 1981), page 55.
6. Howard Hendricks, *Survival in the Ministry* (tape cassette series) (Portland: Multnomah Press, 1981).
7. C. S. Lewis, *The Voyage of the Dawn Treader* (New York: MacMillan, 1952), pages 90-91.
8. Richard Owen Roberts, *Revival* (Wheaton, Illinois: Tyndale House Publishing, 1982), page 25.

CHAPTER FOUR

The Breaking of Bones

. . . the bones which Thou hast broken. . .
Psalm 51:8

For all of us, spiritual growth sometimes means going down a path we would much rather detour around. It means being broken into unstable pieces. But brokenness is a necessary ingredient if we're to go far in Christ. Martin Luther said, "Ah! Affliction is the best book in my library, and let me add, the best leaf in the book of affliction is that blackest of all the leaves, the leaf called heaviness, when the spirit sinks within us and we cannot endure as we would wish."[1]

But brokenness need not always hit with one great blow as it did here in David's life. In fact, if we look closely, we will see incidents and relationships scattered across his life that should have reminded him regularly of his deep dependence on God. His spiritual bones were broken gradually. Whether or not this incident with Bathsheba could have been avoided, from God's perspective, I don't know. But I do know that sometimes the brokenness comes in large bruising doses because we fail to notice the little ways it makes itself felt. It chips away at us so subtly that we don't even realize we're being broken down. Let's take a look at five ways in which people like David, which means people like us, are broken into pieces that can be repaired by God alone.

Relationships are often thorny

Good relationships, the kind David had with Jonathan, are rare but important. They strike necessary blows to the sin that lies within us.

> Now it came about when he had finished speaking to Saul, that the soul of Jonathan was knit to the soul of David, and Jonathan loved him as himself. . . . And Jonathan made David vow again because of his love for him, because he loved him as he loved his own life. (1 Samuel 18:1, 20:17)

The willingness to give, which exists in any close relationship, is a sure antidote to selfishness. The desire to open up and reveal our innermost being to a trusted friend or confidant can thaw a cold defensiveness that locks everyone out. Furthermore, the willingness to receive love can melt us down to a pool of godly humility.

I remember one Father's Day when my son gave me a booklet he had made. In it, there were some amazing insights that touched me deeply. I sat and wept over how undeserving I was to have a wife and children who would love me like that. I will never lose that book. We could all stand a little of that.

Family relationships, both good and bad, by their nature lay us bare, whether we want them to or not. David's family relationships were shaky at best, and could perhaps be typified by a clash with Michal, his wife, described in 2 Samuel 6:20-23. When the Ark of the Covenant was being returned to Jerusalem after being in the hands of the Philistines, the whole city turned out for a festive celebration. And no one was more festive than David, who stripped off his outer garments and danced out in front of the Ark with all his might. When he got home, Michal effectively squashed David's joy by telling him what a fool he'd been by making such a spectacle of himself.

Families can be like that. No one has the capability to hurt us or lift us higher than those we love. The German philosopher Schopenhauer described human relationships as a pack of porcupines on a cold winter's night.[2] They huddle together for warmth, but as soon as they get very close, they jab and hurt each other. So they spend the whole night either huddling or separating.

The withheld opinions and emotions of loved ones can inflict agony within. Intense strife in a relationship can be endured only so long. We eventually find ourselves driven to a heavenly Father when our earthly relationships disappoint us so much. William Carey, the father of modern missions, knew this well.

> The road ahead was not easy. Carey survived a serious attack of malaria, but his little boy Peter did not. Mrs. Carey fell ill again and began to rail against her husband. For weeks he endured her violence against himself and all that he held dear. . . . It was a long time before he realized that her ravings and bitterness were part of her illness. To Carey it seemed that his much-loved Dorothy had become his enemy.[3]

Casual relationships also tend to test our spiritual mettle. Both in our jobs and in the marketplace, we rub shoulders with any number of people whom God uses as sandpaper. Just because the guy next door and the boss are both driving us to the brink of total frustration doesn't mean that the problem is all their fault.

David had an exasperating relationship like this with a man named Joab. Joab was the kind of man many of us are willing to use, even if we don't like him. He not only knew how to get things done; he got results even if honesty and integrity had to be negotiated in the process. Here was the kind of man who could quickly start up a political movement. Although he was loyal to David, he had a fatal flaw: he reserved his fiercest loyalties for himself. His disobeying of orders, deceit, conspiracies, lust for power, and propensity for murder served as a constant aggravation for David, who could never seem to keep control of this aggressive manipulator and power broker.

God allows us to coexist with unethical, difficult, willful people. He uses their offensiveness, irritations, and foibles to drive us to the end of our rope. Then, since we can't escape them, we must use God's resources to cope—with both their shortcomings and our own.

John Wesley and his wife, Molly, had a stormy marriage that affected everyone around them. Charles Wesley, John's brother, never got along with Molly. After enduring one of her tirades, he said, "I must pray or sink into a spirit of revenge."[4] Loving others when there's so much resistance fulfills two purposes. First, the difficult, unlovable people in our world need the love, and second, the unloving person inside our skin needs the practice.

Those eye-to-eye showdowns

King David trusted Nathan, the court prophet. One day, Nathan came to David with a story that made his royal blood boil. There were apparently two men, one rich and one poor. The rich man owned several estates, gigantic herds of sheep and cattle, and had money in the bank to spare. All the poor man had was one little ewe lamb. That little lamb played with his children, ate right from the table, and even curled up to sleep nuzzled against the man's chest. He loved it as if it were his own child.

One day, the rich man had a guest for dinner, but refused to take from his own flocks to provide the meal. Instead, he seized the poor man's ewe lamb and served it to his visitor.

After hearing this report, David seethed! "Anyone who would do such a hideous thing deserves to die!"

David was now ensnared with his own words. "*You* are that man!" Nathan declared. The king's sin was suddenly unmasked. Eye-to-eye with God's prophet, David was reduced to the proper mortal size of a sinner.

Brokenness sometimes invades our lives on the bloody knuckles of confrontation. We desperately need people like Nathan who will tell us the truth, even when it hurts. A myth has grown up around us that if someone really loves us, that person will never hurt our feelings. But if the severe, uncompromising rebukes of Jesus and all the prophets before Him tell us anything, it's that sometimes there are more important things at stake than hurting someone's feelings.

Far more lives have been destroyed because no one spoke up at a crucial moment than because someone was offended by a well-meaning friend. In David's case, the well-being of the people of God was at stake. The integrity and walk with God that was the bedrock of the leadership of Israel had been violated. Eventually the entire nation would suffer.

People who brave the crossfire of your defenses and your ego serve as God's red lights. You ignore them at your own risk. The farther along you are in the Christian life, the harder it sometimes may be to listen to these people, especially if they are younger in the faith, or even nonChristians.

Here's an example. A pastor acquaintance of mine went to his children's school for a conference with their teacher. The teacher commented on the importance of a consistent bedtime and other specific factors that apparently were affecting the performance of these children in the classroom. But he would hear none of it. He was a pastor, a man of God, and everything he did was God's work. Why should he take advice from a nonChristian?

This pastor's kids may end up paying a dear personal price for their father's obstinacy. I also wonder about what spiritual price was paid in this man's sour witness to the teacher.

Sometimes we must go out of our way to get people to tell us the blunt truth about ourselves. Our church elected a standing committee at my request. As pastor, I meet with these men annually for some pointed evaluation of myself and the church, both strengths and weaknesses. If anyone has something to say and is hesitant to come to me, he can go to the committee and know that his concerns will be heard and his anonymity guaranteed. I urge people in all areas of leadership to consider taking the same kind of step, because it probably won't happen unless leaders initiate it. Even if it hurts, we can only grow from such experiences.

Most of us wince a little, at least in spirit, thinking about being on David's end of the confrontation. But as I've grown older, I have a lot more compassion for Nathan. I haven't read much about the price paid by those who must actually do the confronting. I know how heavy that price is. The times when I've played Nathan to someone's David have been some of the blackest days of my life. Some people actually enjoy the confronting role, and their rebuke comes off as a verbal equivalent of the St. Valentine's Day Massacre. But anyone who savors muckraking through someone else's sin just to flex the muscles of his own spiritual pride is guilty of spiritual malpractice.

The one who must confront may be broken on the wheel of many fears. Is this the only way of dealing with the situation? Am I the right one to confront this person? God often has to drag me kicking and screaming to these encounters. I look for every possible alternative and try every excuse to avoid it. But usually I'm either the only one who knows or else the only one who is willing to do something, because others who are aware have chosen to look the other way. There's this strange sensation of being forced to walk down through a tunnel with the walls drawing in tighter as I go. We're finally boxed in, with only one alternative: to confront.

But who am *I* to do this? I certainly have no business playing God, and, besides, there's plenty of sin in my own life that hasn't been mopped up yet. Do I have all the facts necessary for a showdown? The trauma of confrontation will be painful enough, but the possible horror of destroying another person with a false accusation makes me shudder.

Are my hands clean in this? Sometimes the person I must confront has caused me anger and pain. I don't always trust myself to do this with pure motives and without getting in a few shots of my own.

Finally, can I hold the line if the individual won't listen? This is tough. If we're sure that God has led to the confrontation and yet the person balks, we must not back down. To do so would indicate that God has changed His mind about the sin in question, when He has not.

Enduring the presence of someone who at best may be intentionally distant and possibly even hostile isn't easy. And we must do it without becoming proud and gloating about our being right. But it must be done! Leadership has collapsed and whole churches have gone belly-up because everyone was looking the other way or didn't want to hurt somebody's feelings.

Time passes—and carries us in its wake

In 1 Kings 1:1-4, we see David as an old man approaching death. What a mixture of thoughts must have been his as he reflected back upon his life of great achievement with its pockets of deep sorrow. As a young man, his star rose rapidly. Some of us know the feeling, or at least the dream. When we were young we were immortal, and the world was out there waiting to be conquered. But then we encounter the onset of the aging process, and we learn that the world is tougher than it first appeared to be.

The passing of time takes its toll. The accompanying physical changes tend to vent brokenness into our lives. In 1 Kings 1:1-4, we see that David is lying down but that he can't stay warm. Someone gets the idea of choosing a young woman to lie up against him and keep him warm with her body heat. Apparently no one is concerned about anything sexual happening. They all know that a man David's age has lost much of his ability to perform sexually. And David knows it, too. So do many middle-aged men who have extramarital affairs at mid-life, attempting to prove to themselves that they're not losing their sexual function or physical attractiveness.

When our bodies tell us we're getting old, we often do all we can to shut them up. Aging seems to be one of the few sins society still believes in. We have facelifts, hair coloring, and fitness clubs to fight it off. And we would rather not have to look at those who are living reminders that old age is coming no matter what we do.

Are you comfortable around the aged? How do you respond to the toothless old man sitting in a corner drooling, or the senile old lady who doesn't even remember her own children? In not many years, you or I could be one of them.

The deepest reason aging disturbs us is that it marks the way to the inevitability of death. In spite of all we believe about eternal life and heaven, many Christians grapple fiercely and silently with fears of death. I see it when we take prayer requests during our morning worship service. There are always requests for sick loved ones or friends. Inoperable tumors and cancer (especially in young adults with families) bring on a stony silence. Is there any reason why that couldn't be us?

I never used to read obituaries. I do now, taking note of the age at the time of death. The fear that we might die before our kids are grown is real. I want to see their first date, college graduation, wedding day, and on and on. The life God gives us now is rich in many ways that we don't want to lose, even though we will be exchanging them for heaven. Woody Allen once said, "Some men achieve immortality through their work. I want to achieve immortality through not dying." To some degree, he speaks for a lot of us.

Time may not steal just our vitality; it may steal our function, too. For men, in particular, this is a critical danger. As David lay there, he was still officially the king. But others were now making the decisions and carrying out policy, tasks that used to be his. We don't have to wait until we're as far along as David to see this happen. In our forties and fifties, almost all of us will see that some of the expectations we had in our younger days will never be met, some goals never reached. But sometimes letting unmet expectations and goals die, though painful, is necessary so that we can get on with what God has for us.

We can pass through these changes as through doorways into a deeper dependency on God, no matter how aging and death come. Edith Schaeffer tells of a friend named Mr. Van der Weiden who lived in Amsterdam and used his store as a center for the Schaeffers' ministry. Some tests revealed that Mr. Van der Weiden had a malignant brain tumor in an advanced stage. Life was measured in days. Edith Schaeffer describes the scene:

> As Fran and I stood there beside him, gently squeezing his hand for contact and to give unspoken sympathy and communication of loving concern, Mr. Van der Weiden began to speak in jerky and raspy spurts. . . . What he said was easily understood: "Before—I—everything—could— do. Now—I—nothing—can—do." . . . Mr. Van der Weiden was feeling the waste of dying.[5]

All of us will feel at times the waste of dying, both in others and, eventually, in ourselves. As we age and our bodies become infirm and our functioning wanes, it still falls to us to live out each circumstance to the glory of the God who created and redeemed us.

At a local nursing home where I lead worship services lies Pastor Irwin, an old Methodist minister from Tennessee. His wife is dead and he's failing rapidly. Even though he spends most of his time in bed asleep, he always tries to come to the service I lead, where he nods and snores his way through my devotionals.

What can someone like Pastor Irwin still contribute? Although he dozes through much of the service, he never misses the singing, even when he's asleep. Those old hymns that are sung in the country churches of Tennessee rise out of him as if they had a life of their own—which they do when you've loved Jesus Christ for more than seventy-five years. The organ dies and Pastor Irwin stops singing in his sleep.

As they wheel him to his room and I walk to my car, I think of how this dying old man blesses me. Even if he doesn't know I'm there, he shows me the tips of glory that he sees when his heart soars on the wings of those old love songs of the faith. When he's gone, I will never forget the encouragement of seeing a life seasoned so richly with Jesus Christ. There he sits on the threshold of heaven in a nursing home, letting the momentum of the hymns themselves sing him into glory.

How surprised Pastor Irwin will be to awake in eternity and learn what he meant to me. I want the same kind of surprises. You should, too. Trusting God deeply through the transitions of aging and death will go a long way toward making sure that we're not disappointed.

You did *what*?

Great news! The Ark of the Covenant was coming back to Jerusalem! As the procession entered the city, no one was more exultant than David. He was so filled with joy that he couldn't hold it in. So he didn't. Wrapping himself in nothing but a linen girdle, David ran ahead of the Ark, dancing for all he was worth (2 Samuel 6:14-20). Not everyone else was quite as thrilled as David. After all, kings aren't supposed to act like that. They should try to maintain their public image with dignity, shouldn't they? Or should they?

And what about the dignity of clergymen? Our church had a guest speaker in for a week of services. Both in his preaching and in his dealing with individuals, I was impressed with his discernment and sensitivity. At the end of the week when we were alone, I felt compelled to ask him to evaluate our ministry, since we were still relatively new. He gave it to me straight: "These people have responded to God working through you. They want to love you, but you won't let them in." He was right. But even though I knew God was using this man to get my attention about something vital to my ministry, where could I start? Then it hit me.

The next Sunday I was concluding my sermon with a few remarks about the services the week before. I said, "God dealt deeply with me and I want to share it with you." With that I unknotted my tie, pulled it off, and put it on the seat behind me. If a few eyebrows went up then, the rest blew off the top of the chart when I did the same with my coat and vest!

As I started to unbutton my shirt, I explained, "God has told me that I'm becoming something I loathe: a mere clergyman, a religious professional. You have tried to show me your love in my first year, but I haven't let you in. You ought to know who I am down deep before you decide that loving me is worth it. Here's what I am."

As I said this, I undid the last button. The entire place was as quiet as a tomb as I peeled off my shirt and let it fall to the floor—revealing the black and gold of the Pittsburgh Steelers! The place fell apart. It was a wonderful catharsis. We laughed. We hugged and we cried. A bonding started that Sunday that has continued until today. But I'm certain that it wouldn't have come off had I not taken that dramatic first step.

While there is no inherent virtue in weirdness per se, I think that just about every Christian could greatly enhance his or her witness to a lost world by loosening up a little. I can see why Jesus was drawn to children; adults can be pretty boring people. We incorporate dignity of the wrong sort into our Christian life— becoming stoical and reserved to a lifeless extreme.

In Mark Twain's *Tom Sawyer,* Tom describes an argument with crotchety, church-going Aunt Polly over heaven and hell. Tom ends things by saying that he would rather go to the bad place because he couldn't see any sense in going where Aunt Polly was going!

God doesn't follow *our* lead. *He's* the leader! And He leads people to do all kinds of eccentric, unpredictable things that seem to make no sense. He grants a child to a lady named Sarah, who is way past childbearing age. He leads Hosea, one of His prophets, to marry a prostitute. Peter and John, after taking a severe beating for preaching the gospel, walk down the street singing praises to God at the top of their lungs. Paul and Silas sit in a prison, of all places, singing praises through most of the night—without an organ.

If we were as fiercely concerned about God's dignity as we are about our own, we would be much better off. Much of the so-called reverence displayed in our churches fits the Pharisees better than Jesus. God has never committed Himself to upholding our dignity. In fact, He'll strip it all away, if necessary.

Two good barometers for recognizing people fierce for God's dignity are laughter and tears. Christians who never have the laughter of joy, especially when together with others, are a living tragedy. The sharpest rebuke against my own dryness I've ever experienced has been the true joy and laughter of Christians in the midst of serious suffering. How often is laughter heard in the various areas of your life, and why? A vibrant Christian life is peppered with it.

Tears are usually even more scarce than laughter. That many floors of churches have never absorbed the tears of Christians is tragic. Many of us, men in particular, have lost the ability to cry. As I speak with people about how they came to Christ, I find that many have received the gift of tears.

R. W. Dale, a noted pastor of the last century, told how he was initially unimpressed by D. L. Moody, until the day he sat on the platform and watched Moody preach. Dale became convinced of Moody's sincerity, saying, "He could never speak of a lost soul without tears in his eyes."[6]

Pulpits and pews should see more tears over both the joy of

our redemption and the sorrow of our need for more spiritual depth with the Lord. There is definitely no place for a Christian to be fueled by his emotions, but neither is there a place for him to deny them.

It comes down to a choice. We can't be fiercely dedicated both to God's dignity and reputation, and to our own. We take ourselves far too seriously. This example of a humble missionary provides a sound model for us:

A close friend had just returned to the United States on furlough from missions service in Latin America. He had earned two undergraduate degrees, a master's degree, and a doctorate from the same university. He had taken his family to Colombia to live in a jungle for ten years among a forgotten, isolated group of people.

My friend told a group of businessmen that his alma mater was about to celebrate its 100th anniversary and wanted to publish a book to share the work of its outstanding graduates. One day an airplane circled his little jungle clearing and delivered his "air mail" by throwing out a packet attached to a small parachute that floated down into the jungle. He found in the packet a letter from his university with a series of questions.

The first was: "Do you own your own home?" He thought back to the days when he and his friends had built this two-room house out of the jungle for $100. So he checked "yes." Question two: "Do you own two homes?" "No" was his first reaction, but then he recalled that Jesus said, "I go to prepare a place for you, that where I am you may be also." So he checked "yes." Question three was: "Do you own a boat?" He looked out to the river below his house and saw the forty-foot canoe he and his friends had hollowed out of a log with the little outboard motor on it and answered "yes." Question four asked: "Do you plan to travel abroad this year?" He called to his wife in the other room, "Margaret, are we going home on furlough this year?"

She answered, "Yes." So again he answered affirmatively. The final question was: "What is your annual salary?" He searched down the list of suggested salary figures which began at $250,000 and could not find a figure to match his missionary quota. So he drew a line across the bottom of the list and wrote the very small amount of salary he was receiving.

After telling this story, my friend leaned over, and with a sparkle in his eye said, "When I leave you, I am heading out to the West Coast and will visit my alma mater. I just can't wait to get out there and see what I did to the computers!"[7]

A voice that won't go away

For a select group of people, brokenness must be especially deep. These are the ones who have had a special calling from God but have refused to obey. It may have been to the ministry or to missions. The lure of money and career, a relationship (usually a marriage one), or something else has led these people to defy God at the center of their being in a major decision. Like Jonah, they hear God's call, and then turn away.

Such individuals usually attempt to compensate through one of three strategies. One is avoidance: dropping completely out of Christian circles. Many never return. All of us remember Christians of initial zeal and fire, who flounder at some point of commitment and are suddenly lost to Christ's cause.

A second way out is pseudo-endurance: trying to co-exist with the barest minimum of the faith. This category of people goes to church. Possibly they're regular attenders. Having tasted the good things of Christ, they cannot rationalize totally staying away. The lingering conviction of a mistake they have worked subconsciously to bury would be too strong. But while they may attend church, actual worship is impossible. Every second in a church building is a muted reminder of a loving God defied in a moment of selfishness. They mumble the hymns, stare out the window or at the floor, and are the first ones out the door. Amazingly, some manage to continue this religious charade the rest of their lives. Many drop out. Thankfully, some return to God.

A third group warrants careful attention. These not only attend church, but they ascend into leadership. This may seem strange, but not really. These people often fill positions of leadership, but they are usually spiritually ineffective. Good spiritual leaders are called and gifted, but these people ran away from all that long ago. Being effective isn't their top priority anyway; being right and being in control is.

These are the people who muzzle, suffocate, and split churches. Because they're contentious, they lead through intimidation, sometimes of the most subtle kind. Outbursts of anger, threats about leaving the church, or intimations of withdrawing financial support, make opponents retreat quickly. I've even seen one man who could get his way without a word. Giving the appearance of extraordinary sensitivity, his face could take on the most hurt expression at crucial moments. He effectively controlled all church policy, since no one would think of hurting his feelings by opposing him.

For this third category of God-evaders, getting their own way means being in control. They are in the driver's seat, which means, according to their selfishly twisted view, that they are doing a good job in God's work. A person needs to be convinced that he has something really good if he's going to offer his service in the flesh as a bribe to God to overlook a forgone calling in his past. "Look," he'll rationalize, "this is just as good as that opportunity back there was, isn't it? Let's just forget it."

Some people are far more adamant. They'll fight God to the death. Their leadership in the church has become the arena where they will prove God wrong by showing that what they're doing now is as good, if not better, than what He had in mind years ago. Dying is almost a preferable alternative to admitting that an entire lifetime has been lived according to the wrong agenda.

There is a way back to God for all three of these who have heard His call and walked away. We must go deliberately back to the point of disobedience, admit that we were wrong, and then confess to why we did it. This may hurt unbelievably, but we can do it. The Holy Spirit will help us. Three things may result.

For the first time in years we will be able to experience peace with God. Isn't this alone worth it? None of these people, regardless of their response, is at peace with God. No one can enjoy God and His favors and then walk away without becoming impoverished for it.

Second, God may reissue the call. Miraculously enough, the opportunity may not be totally gone, and although it may cost more (a lucrative career left behind, a daring and uncertain future, etc.), we may still have the privilege of serving in that original calling.

Third, there is the possibility that God may issue a new call. Some opportunities are lost forever. But a forgiven life taken out of the spiritual mothballs can glorify God in new opportunities of His choosing.

We have just looked at five major ways in which people become broken within. This quintet is scattered across everyone's life in one way or another. If we are willing to listen carefully, they will constantly remind us of our need to completely rely on God. Possibly we'll save ourselves the trauma of a major spiritual blowout such as the one David suffered.

But although David learned the hard way, he did learn. The rest of this book catalogs from Psalm 51 all the losses resulting from his sin, losses that David was so sadly aware of. Christians everywhere sustain the same kinds of losses—*but* there is good news! No matter how broken we become, God can put all the pieces back together again. He alone can make us whole. But we must play our part, too. Our incentive is that all *can* be restored. David made it through his brokenness with a renewed spirit. We, too, can experience a renaissance within.

NOTES:
1. Charles H. Spurgeon, *New Park Street Pulpit, 1858,* Volume 4 (London: Banner of Truth Trust, 1964), pages 400-461.
2. David Watson, *I Believe in the Church* (Grand Rapids: William B. Eerdmans Publishing Co., 1978), page 367.
3. John Pollock, *Victims of the Long March* (Waco, Texas: Word Books, 1970), page 16.
4. William J. Peterson, *Martin Luther Had a Wife* (Wheaton: Tyndale House Publishers, 1983), page 62.
5. Edith Schaeffer, *Affliction* (Old Tappan, N. J.: Fleming H. Revell, 1978), pages 67-68.
6. John R. W. Stott, *Between Two Worlds: The Art of Preaching in the Twentieth Century* (Grand Rapids: Eerdmans, 1982), page 276.
7. David Howard, ed., *Declare His Glory* (Downers Grove, Illinois: InterVarsity Press, 1977), pages 35-36.

CHAPTER FIVE

The Striptease of Sin

*Behold, Thou dost desire truth
in the innermost being,
And in the hidden part Thou
wilt make me know wisdom.*
Psalm 51:6

■

Have you ever seen a striptease? Walking down the street in a large city a group of us passed one of those strip joints. A television monitor was mounted over the door showing a continuous parade of young ladies to be found inside. Bunched together on the sidewalk, a crowd had gathered to stare. In fact there were so many that we had to step into the street to pass by. I have a feeling that anyone paying to get in was disappointed.

Temptation is the striptease of sin. In seducing our hearts, it promises satisfaction and fulfillment that never genuinely materializes in the way originally anticipated. One thing is promised, another is delivered. Temptation may be alluring, but sin always exacts a price for that shallow come-on.

Most Christians already understand this. After all, doesn't Romans 6:23 say that "the wages of sin is death"? And Ezekiel 18:4 promises that "the soul who sins will die." But we often have a seat-belt mentality toward sin. Most of us know we should use

59

seat belts, but since accidents always seem to happen to other people, it's nothing to drive off without buckling up. It's one thing to believe we must rely on Christ's death for the forgiving of our sins and quite another to live daily according to that belief.

After all, we're not so bad—certainly not any worse than lots of other people we could think of. If this attitude sounds like us, then we need to rethink the idea of death. Sin is one investment that doesn't rely solely on deferred dividends. It simply doesn't wait until eternity to pay off. Death is much more than the end of life. It's a hideous object lesson on our separation from God that always results from sin. This separation is gradual, draining, and debilitating. It cheats us of qualities of soul and character that only the genuine forgiveness found in Jesus Christ can restore. As we continue to examine Psalm 51, the rest of this book will focus on not only the erosive effects of sin but also the hope of restoration.

It's nobody's business but my own

Sin can cheat us of our innermost integrity. Have you ever invested in the myth of the compartmentalized life? Its basic premise is that we can live our private lives any way we like, as long as our public and professional lives remain unaffected. Old Testament sages would sadly shake their heads to think that people like us—as modern and sophisticated as we like to believe we are—could think such a thing. The heart of man is not a series of adjoining airtight compartments. Man is a whole, a unity. "Above all else, guard your heart, for it is the wellspring of life" (Proverbs 4:23, NIV). What we are in our hearts inevitably affects what we do.

If we need convincing, David can teach us a lot. A person who is wrapped up in sensuality is usually unapproachable, saying, "Look, it's my life. As long as it doesn't overflow into my job, it really isn't anyone else's business." But is that really true?

It was because of David's position that his sin was compounded. It was because of his authority that he could command

Bathsheba to be brought to his bed chamber. That same authority made it possible for him to manipulate Bathsheba's husband, who served him faithfully. David's position as commander in chief made the murder of Uriah very easy to arrange, when all other attempts at a cover-up failed. And finally, his respected position intimidated him into hastily arranging a marriage to conceal an out-of-wedlock pregnancy.

David's integrity was thoroughly shattered. Crying out of spiritual hindsight, David said to God, "Surely you desire truth in the inner parts" (Psalm 51:6, NIV). Stinging under the guilt of sin, which had raped him of his integrity, David learned too late that the bedrock of solid character is established not in position but in truth—pure, open honesty in word and deed. The implications of this kind of compromise of integrity are at least threefold.

The end before the means
First, the end never justifies the means—*never*. Certainly not when that means is sinful. Principle, not mere results, should determine our actions as Christians at all times—no exceptions. In view of our orthodox beliefs, institutional growth, and financial success in the church, the powerlessness of so many Christians is a perplexing thing. But has it ever occurred to us that God may not necessarily be pleased with visible results alone? David certainly had all the visible success anyone could want, yet God judged him fearfully.

Carelessness in the area of motives will inevitably paralyze us, for then the spinal cord of power could be severed. Whenever principles become obscured in a pragmatic desire for results, we need to ask ourselves some probing questions about whose kingdom we are really building. All David's energies were concentrated on getting what he wanted and protecting his reputation. We might do well to ask ourselves where *our* energies are concentrated.

One of the best places to hide these tendencies to put the cart before the horse—the end before the means—is under the guise of serving God. The attraction to sacrifice motives and means for results has never been as strong for me as it has been since I've been a pastor. Few people have much of an idea what a pastor does between Sundays. Many pastors resort to a full schedule of meetings and activities in an attempt to justify their presence in the eyes of their people. These men feel trapped. Others do the same thing with an eye toward enhancing their own reputation. The record high attendance in Sunday school last week doesn't necessarily feed my ego. It merely "underscores my pastoral authority in the eyes of my people."

Who are we kidding? Maybe we've pulled the wool over the eyes of a lot of the trusting people in the church for the time being. But we're certainly not kidding God, who shares glory with no one and demands truth in the inner parts of *all* His followers.

Even reading the mail can be an intimidating experience for me. The newsletter from the church down the street that's growing faster than we are gets read and thrown away first. Then I sit over coffee with the pastor of that church, nodding with an ambiguous grin while he gives me all the details. I know what it is to recolor, recast, and inflate what is going on in our church in self-defense. I come away feeling dirty.

Self-worship under the guise of serving God always has that kind of effect. When principles are openly violated, either to keep the machinery running as smoothly as possible or to make ourselves look good without regard for the rape of human and material resources, we are sitting in David's seat. Sadly, we fit it all too well.

I'm as good as anyone else

Another implication of compromise of character is the tendency to judge ourselves against others, especially those people who have the most blatant problems with sin. The standard for our principles should be neither the world nor the Christian community. Our standard is the Word of God. If we establish this high standard in our lives, then we will not be so ready to compromise in the face of temptation. Compromise and comparison have become an expedient part of living in the world that the Christian community is infected with. Leaders at all levels, including elected church leaders, become power brokers, sinning openly without reprimand. They are sanctimonious, unapproachable, and unbroken. As long as people and money keep rolling in, everything is fine. But fine according to whom?

It's so easy to be lulled into a false sense of security. There are always the defeats and struggles of other Christians for our pride to feed on. Since we seem to be at least on a spiritual par with those around us, we must be doing well enough. But other people and other churches are not the standard. When God's Word ceases to be our standard, our sense of His will is numbed and we succumb to what could be called a sin binge. Many dieters do so well for a while—just long enough to feel successful. To reward themselves, they cheat on their diet and binge, thus ruining everything they had accomplished.

David had experienced victories and successes in all areas of his life. Victories, especially spiritual ones, can be rather intoxicating. But when we're living on the heights, we can allow what seems to be a minor shift in standards, and all of a sudden we've lost our perspective. We forget who God is. He strangely begins to resemble us. And so the stage is set for people who know and love God to do foolish, sinful things.

The compromise of integrity

A third aspect of compromise in the face of temptation is the loss of our inner spiritual zeal and integrity. God demands of His people a "belly-to-backbone" honesty—truth in the inward parts. Have you ever read John 8? It has always impressed me as a chapter to be read only while wearing an asbestos suit. Here is one of the fieriest encounters Jesus ever had with the Pharisees. Before the chapter ends, they have accused Him twice of being demon possessed and are on the verge of making an attempt on His life. Jesus says to those religious pretenders, "Which one of you convicts Me of sin? If I speak truth, why do you not believe Me?" (John 8:46).

Would we be able to confidently ask our enemies that question? Here Jesus is throwing down the gauntlet to His opponents and challenging them to publicly discredit Him—if they can. He is staking the authenticity of His entire ministry not on the results of the ministry but on the integrity of His character. Integrity steeped in the truth of God's Word is the steel framework of a person's soul. It's the stock in trade of a Christian's life, keeping him inwardly strong when he is confronted by temptation. When our integrity is compromised, the ringing of the gospel is muted.

The Christians are few and far between who haven't asked God to use them in some way. I sure have—sometimes boldly when my love for God waxes impassioned with an ardent spirit. But more often, I ask God to use me only as a weak afterthought, just wanting an emotional lift when the tide is out, while demands press in upon me and drudgery suffocates my spiritual fire. Regardless of why we ask, are we the kind of persons who can be trusted with a deeper walk or a wider service? Is there truth in the inward parts? This is more than a matter of raw honesty.

Honesty by itself can be brutal. In college, I knew a fellow who had earned a reputation for being tactless and rude. One day he told me his story. Somehow lying had become ingrained in him as a young child and plagued him all through his school years. He carried within him constantly the hidden fear of being found out. He said, "Dave, you'll never know how good it feels to just tell the truth." But he overreacted. Although he now told the truth, he did so without tact and sensitivity. Many people around him were hurt needlessly.

God's truth in the inner parts is an integrity that blooms when honesty is liberally seasoned with grace. It means being willing to stand straight when standing straight isn't popular. It holds true when no crowd is there to applaud, and delights in playing to the audience of God alone.

Life against the grindstone

David keenly felt the wounding of his integrity, and so he cherished the hope that God would use what had happened to instill wisdom within him. David said, "You teach me wisdom in the inmost place" (Psalm 51:6, NIV).

Wisdom is the acquired ability to live life well. It's living life against the grindstone and coming away polished instead of being chewed up. It's when our mistakes and failures become our teachers. And today it is in both strong demand and short supply. The number of professing Christians who divorce, have nervous breakdowns, and commit suicide is rising. And the tougher it gets to cope, the more tempting it is to want to escape or hide. In the church, this epidemic of spiritual withdrawal is one of the best kept secrets around.

> Our churches are filled with people who outwardly look contented and at peace but inwardly are crying out for someone to love them . . . just as they are—confused, frustrated, often frightened, guilty and often unable to communicate even within their own families. But the *other* people in the church *look* so happy and contented that one seldom has the courage to admit his own deep needs before such a self-sufficient group as the average church meeting appears to be.[1]

The wisdom needed in silently desperate lives such as these would require a combination of keen discernment and practical common sense (Proverbs 8:1-5,32-36). True wisdom begins with a healthy, not craven, fear of God (Proverbs 9:10). Our sense of awe and fear of God needs to grip us constantly, shaking us free of our pretense and insecurity.

God's holiness in all its fierce intensity is shown in the Cross of Christ. Sin could not be allowed to do its hideous work unchecked. God took on flesh and pressed the fight on sin's own ground, stopping nothing short of spilling His own blood. There was no peaceful coexistence, no mutual disarmament. Two old foes glared at one another across eternity, knowing there could never be an end until one of them lay face down in the dust, never again to rise.

There are at least two reasons why there isn't more wisdom available as a balm to soothe our wounded lives, as a lubricant when life rubs us raw. First, our beliefs are often shallow and cheaply held. Dorothy Sayers rightly commented that people who would be horrified at the account of a cat killing a bird can hear the story of the killing of God told Sunday after Sunday with no real sense of shock at all. A lot of our evangelical belief is file folder stuff. We have all the right information tucked away, but that's about all it is—just the right information. The ring of reality and the impact of truth is not there.

Second, we have a tendency to become evasive when the things we say we believe come too close for comfort. When sin stops being a cold, abstract doctrine and stands there in front of us pointing a finger, it often finds us conveniently looking the other way. But as a prod toward wisdom, Paul warns us in the Word of God very clearly.

> Count yourselves dead to sin but alive to God in Christ Jesus. Therefore do not let sin reign in your mortal body so that you obey its evil desires. Do not offer the parts of your body to sin, as instruments of wickedness, but rather offer yourselves to God, as those who have been brought from death to life; and offer the parts of your body to him as instruments of righteousness. (Romans 6:11-13, NIV)

It is one thing to believe that something is dangerous. But we need to actually act upon that danger warning.

A man was once cutting wood. Stepping over a log, he heard the raspy warning of a small rattlesnake. The obvious response would have been to back away, letting the snake move off. But the woodcutter decided that it would be just as easy to kill the snake with the saw. That was his mistake. Throwing the switch, he easily cut the snake's head off but the spinning chain threw the severed head against the man's leg, where the fangs of the still-opened mouth stuck like darts. The man was as snake bitten as he would have been had the snake been alive in one piece. Is the power of sin broken? Yes, but even a dead snake can give a lethal bite.

David learned that same basic lesson the hard way. He had succumbed to the alluring sirens of temptation, and then dug himself in deeper by trying to cover up his sin with more of the same. David was bitten by a spiritual snake, but, due to the warning and grace of God, he recognized what he had to do. He needed to act immediately to take the appropriate measures to keep the venom from totally destroying him.

Although David learned the hard way, often the hard way can be the very best way to make sure you never forget. Sin that's been confessed, wrestled with, and overcome is one of the finest teachers we can have. Our struggles and defeats can increase our spiritual growth just as much as our victories—*if* we learn from them.

That is the primary value of this story about David. The Bible is filled with reports of many others like him. No fairy tales or ivory towers there. This is reality. The Bible speaks candidly of people who were quite familiar with the jostles and assaults of everyday life. The hard knocks of life and the venomous stings of sin deeply marked the people whose life stories are recorded in Scripture.

But instead of being totally devastated by the insidious conspiracy of temptation and sin, people like David seem to emerge seasoned and polished. They know that the saccharine veneer of sin has a bitter core. And how is it that the poisoning process is not only halted but reversed? How can anyone grow through temptations, trials, and even the ravages of deep sin? We can all grow through our scars and brokenness because of the counsel, comfort, and healing of the God who uses all things—yes, even the desolate aftermath following sin—to bring us back to our spiritual senses and back to Him.

David's hope was for the kind of wisdom that would refine him through the spiritual fire. This same hope and commitment should be ours. Otherwise, sin that still masters us teaches us nothing. It enslaves. The striptease of sin keeps teasing and promising what it cannot deliver. For no wisdom is gleaned, and what begins as a striptease becomes a spiritual rape.

NOTES:
1. Keith Miller, *The Taste of New Wine* (Waco: Word Publishers, 1965), page 22.

CHAPTER SIX

Dancing with Broken Bones

Purify me with hyssop, and I shall be clean;
Wash me, and I shall be whiter than snow.
Make me to hear joy and gladness,
Let the bones which Thou hast broken rejoice.
Hide Thy face from my sins,
And blot out all my iniquities.
Psalm 51:7-9

■

When I was a teenager, I met a *Playboy* magazine "Playmate of the Year." She was making a promotional appearance at a nearby mall. So my friends and I went. We found a line at least a hundred yards long snaking through the mall. After what seemed like hours, I finally stepped up to the table where she was sitting. But nothing could have prepared me for what I saw there. Was she beautiful? Yes, she was a stunning Scandinavian blond. But that wasn't what startled me so much that I hesitated when she asked my name.

These ladies are portrayed as people who enjoy the good life. They're attractive and rising rapidly in their professions. They winter at Aspen and summer on the Riviera. All the juices of life flow freely and the sky is the limit.

That's why I was so shocked. I was expecting something different in her eyes—perhaps some glow or sparkle. But as I looked into her eyes, I was shocked. I had never seen an emptier, more meaningless gaze. How could someone who apparently had so much going for her be so inwardly barren and destitute that it showed on her face?

I've never forgotten the wasteland in her eyes. I never will. She was as stripped of human vitality and joy as an ear of corn shucked of its husk and grain. I wish I could say that hers was the last of the vacant stares I've ever seen, but I'm afraid I've seen many since then. That empty, soul-drained look is everywhere. What is especially dismaying is the frequency with which it is found within the church.

Sour saints

How is it that people become so somber? How many people do you know who are enjoying their Christian life? I mean people who are savoring their relationship with God regardless of the externals. Even thinking this way is foreign to us. In times when many people believe that honor can be upheld only at a distance and that respect never roots well in the soil of intimacy, the suggestion to enjoy the Christian life sounds rather utopian or naive.

So many of us seem as though we must have been baptized in vinegar. We get so spiritually pinched and tight that it almost seems like we have to get up in the morning to tell bad news instead of good news. The sour, stoical joylessness of so many Christians has a spiritually suffocating influence. It not only smothers a penetrating witness to a secular society but also at times makes that society seem more attractive by comparison than what Christ is offering.

But the contrasting fact is that nothing is more attractive than a life saturated with a personal knowledge of Jesus Christ. We should carefully note that in Psalm 51, one of the first things David asked to have restored was joy. Without it, our lives and our witness are flat and tasteless. Our eyes take on that soul-drained look.

No substitutes allowed

The significance of David's petition for joy is easily lost on our late twentieth-century minds. We've struck an easy compromise with two incompatible bedfellows. Many lives are controlled by either a shallow emotionalism or a self-sufficient stoicism. Being at the mercy and whim of superficial, ever-changing feelings is a tough and exhausting way to live. But so is the option of denying all emotion, padlocking our hearts, and living under a veneer of ever-vigilant self-control. Sadly, many of us Christians have mastered both, and can dance from one to the other with amazing dexterity. In the process, our capacity to feel deeply is numbed. God's presence is sensed only when emotion is stimulated to a level that is impossible to maintain.

David is all at once sitting on the bottom rung of the ladder, a place we avoid as much as possible. We tend to lust for a state of rapture and thrive on positive strokes. We ignore the spiritual reality that when we have a broken heart and a contrite spirit we become pliable in the hands of God. This process of brokenness is almost always painful. A. W. Tozer so rightly said, "It is highly doubtful that God can use a man significantly until he has hurt deeply."

At a glance, verses 7-9 of Psalm 51 seem similar to the first two verses. Although much of the language is the same, these later verses are embellished with unique word pictures. This is more than a variation of style. In Scripture, as in other works of literature, word pictures can be a hint of intensity. Books like Daniel and Revelation are good examples. Both were initially written for God's people under duress. When the pressure has been great and the suffering severe, God has used artists who can paint whole vistas with a pen.

Genuine prayer often reveals the same kind of picture-painting process. Much of our language in prayer, on the contrary, is usually so vague and dull that even if God is able to untangle it, He must wonder how badly we want our request. It drones heavily in the air like the sluggish buzzing of the last housefly infesting our home before the onset of winter. Compare this with another one of David's prayers to the Lord in Psalm 139:

> How precious . . . are Thy thoughts to me, O God!
> How vast is the sum of them!
> If I should count them, they would outnumber the sand.
> When I awake, I am still with Thee. . . .
> Search me, O God, and know my heart;
> Try me and know my anxious thoughts;
> And see if there be any hurtful way in me,
> And lead me in the everlasting way.
> (Psalm 139:17-18, 23-24)

This is just a small sample of the urgency, along with the beauty, in word images David speaks forth to the Lord in Psalm 139. While I don't recommend this as a model, it does show the vivid language that often comes with urgency. When a pint of language won't hold a gallon of meaning, word pictures say a lot.

What did David want so badly after he was confronted by God's representative, Nathan? He asked God to "purify," to purge him (Psalm 51:7). What he was literally asking of God in the Hebrew language was, "Un-sin me."[1]

David wanted to be clean to the very core of his being. No minor reform or substitute would do. Only a complete transformation would satisfy his craving. David's word for "wash" here in verse 7 gives the picture of dirty clothes being pounded on a rock. This works fine with dirty socks, but gets rather tough on human lives. But David thought it was worth it. He had to regain the joy of knowing God no matter what the cost. A recent song says it well:

> Whatever it takes to get closer to You, Lord,
> that's what I'll be willing to do.

For whatever it takes to be more like You,
    that's what I'll be willing to do.
I'll trade sunshine for rain, comfort for pain,
    that's what I'll be willing to do.
Whatever it takes for my will to break,
    that's what I'll be willing to do.[2]

David longed to be clean again and to taste the joy only that kind of spiritually laundered state could bring. But the kind of joy David desired was much more than just a passing whisk of a sponge, much more than a flurry of emotions. That kind of quick fix is so tempting, isn't it? Crushed by circumstances and sorrow or wincing under the bitter taste of plodding spiritual barrenness, the longing for a gushing purge of happiness is strong. But in the thick of the doldrums, it's always easier to know our wants better than our needs.

Looking back at some very dusty times in my own life, I now realize that all I really wanted was an emotional icebreaker to make myself feel better—far more than I wanted Jesus Christ. I still haven't outrun the pull of that need, and probably never will. I need a sign post. Maybe you do, too. There are plenty of people who cannot sense God's presence at all without strong emotional surges, and many of them lie constantly crippled by a fixation on feelings.

David can help us in this area if we will listen. Not joy alone but the joy of *salvation* was the prize. Untarnished intimacy with God must be rooted in a transparent honesty that starts at the Cross of Jesus Christ.

Have you ever had a broken bone? Firing out excruciating signals of pain, a broken bone really gets your undivided attention. The pain is bad enough, but note carefully in this passage that this is pain caused by *God*: "Let the bones which Thou hast broken rejoice" (Psalm 51:8). How can a loving God deliberately inflict pain, especially on one of His own people? Simply, David paints here one of the most vivid portraits of conviction of sin in the Bible. His broken bones were not physical, but spiritual.

The Spirit is not silent
It almost seems that the Holy Spirit is being rediscovered after a long period of neglect. Crossing denominational lines, Christians are finding ever deeper relationships with Christ. This should be good news. But if we say we want all that the Spirit has for us, we should weigh our words carefully, for He will inevitably unwrap one gift guaranteed to melt our shallow, self-seeking smiles away: conviction of sin. Does that astonish and disturb us? It shouldn't. Jesus promised that this would be one of the most notable marks of the Spirit's presence.

Jesus said, "When [the Spirit] comes, he will convict the world of guilt in regard to sin and righteousness and judgment" (John 16:8, NIV). The Lord also promised that the Spirit would come to indwell believers (John 14:16-17), reveal the things of God (John 14:26), and testify of Christ (John 16:13-15). When Jesus promised all these things, He wasn't just holding them up as options for us to pick and choose according to our own whim. The Holy Spirit is a divine Person with an undivided nature. To have God's Spirit living in us is to be indwelt by One who will never peacefully coexist with sin. This is a greatly needed corrective for a growing number of people who believe they can be Spirit-filled while leading down-in-the-gutter kinds of lives!

But how much pain is necessary for us to come to our spiritual senses? Sinclair Ferguson writes pointedly, "The best answer is: whatever depth and length of conviction will draw us to faith in Christ. Degrees of conviction will differ just as believers do themselves. It is impossible to offer a general prescription, or even to judge in advance of the operations of the Holy Spirit."[3]

But we need to be careful. Feeling guilty isn't the same as actually being guilty. Satan is the relentless accuser of the brethren (Revelation 12:10), and he does it so well! Christians paralyzed with guilt over things that are not even sinful, or over sin that has already been confessed, are just so many notches on his smoking gun. How do we sort it out? How can new Christians or more seasoned offenders tell the Spirit's pricking from Satan's slander? David knew the difference. So can we if we ponder carefully David's choice of words.

A cold rain is splattering and running down my window as I'm writing. I love the coming cold, but not the flu season it will bring. Most of us have experienced the onslaught of the flu leaving us feeling wrung out, with a body ache that hurts everywhere but nowhere in particular. This gives us a faint idea what Satan's false charges are like. Negative phrases sifting through the mind, such as "You're no good!" or "How can Christ use you?" leave us wallowing in a feeling of uselessness, weakness, and self-pity. The mocking undercurrent of this kind of inner turmoil does nothing but deepen our feelings of alienation.

David chose the picture of broken bones to describe the pain a person experiences when God is dealing with the human spirit. With broken bones, the pain is sharp and specific, and we feel compelled to do anything necessary to take care of the problem. Satan's accusing is usually ambiguous, mocking, debilitating, and alienating. The Spirit's conviction is specific, is based on Scripture, and draws us compellingly back to reconciliation through confession.

Joy and intimacy

The New English Bible translates the last half of verse eight in a delightful way: "Let the bones dance which thou hast broken." Dancing with broken bones is a rare and beautiful art form in the spiritual realm. But joy is devalued currency among us, and we show it. True joy is more than an emotion. It is one of the fruits of the Holy Spirit, and is a delicate but hardy blossom. Fueled by the Spirit, it can exist alongside crushing negative emotions, actually in spite of them. Elizabeth Skoglund wisely writes:

In an era of "Praise the Lord" theology, the real meaning of words like praise and joy may become lost to superficiality. For it is only in deep suffering that people know the depths of all emotion, whether it be pain that is almost unbearable even for one moment more or joy that sweeps over the soul once that pain is gone. On an even more profound level, joy can exist with pain if one accurately defines that joy.[4]

Do things really have to be going my way all the time for me to know joy? All my problems solved? All my anxieties extinguished? If so, then we've saddled our joys to some cheap mounts. Another one of God's great ironies of truth is that His joy is tied not to circumstances but to Himself. Even pain can be a ladder to joy if both the pain and joy are rightly understood.

For example, a truly loving God disciplines His children *because* He loves them, just as any conscientious parent takes action when it is appropriate (Hebrews 12:5-11). Whether our trials come clearly from God or through unclear channels in our lives, they are all potential means to spiritual growth.[5] Pains of conviction, failure, and discipline all amazingly wind their way back to the joy of knowing God, who goes beyond forgiveness and restoration to do amazing new work in our lives.

True joy is more than a passing emotion. It's the natural overflow of a life in union with the God who both created it and redeemed it. It was never meant to hang on the hooks of the circumstances of our lives—the results of the x-rays, the kids' next report cards, or the blister on the bottom of my left foot. Rather, it's amazing stuff that blazes up most strongly when I am weak or have the least reason to feel it. Joy is an incredibly satisfying thing that lays bedrock in a person's soul, something that can't be shaken. Too many have tasted too little of it. Why is that?

Our joylessness is a symptom of something deeply wrong. We do not understand, and therefore do not appreciate, intimacy.

We gossip away the privacies of others' lives merely to satisfy our craven appetite for the attention of our peers. At every cash register in America, the journals of "supermarket scholarship" leer at us and jump into our baskets. Intimacy with other people and with God is almost an unknown thing for a lot of us.

Paul says to all believers, "You did not receive a spirit that makes you a slave again to fear, but you received the Spirit of sonship. And by him we cry, '*Abba*, Father'" (Romans 8:15, NIV). Most of us believe this just enough to take it for granted, instead of taking it to heart. Intimacy with God. We presumptuously expect Him to know us. But that we should be growing into a close, ongoing personal relationship with Him seems almost improper, an undue familiarity bordering on the sacrilegious. Actually, it's a treasure and a trust not to be surrendered lightly or thrown indiscriminately to the pandering public eye.

While I was in college, a businessman took a number of us under his wing. Mel led a Bible study in our apartment. Our respect for that man couldn't have been greater. Quite simply, Mel knew God. We knew there must have been some great spiritual experiences he had gone through along the way, so we decided to ask about a few. All of us settled in for some good "ghost stories" as we popped our request on him. I'll never forget his reply. He said, "The Lord and I have had some special times together, but they are not for retelling. They're too personal."

Over the past several years, I've grown to see the wisdom in his reply. Although personal testimony has its place, not every experience should be shared publicly. There's an interesting allusion in 1 Corinthians 15:5: about the risen Christ appearing to Peter. The same incident is hinted at in Luke 24:34. But you won't find the slightest clue as to what was said in that private conversation. The "scandal sheets" didn't have a photographer hiding in the bushes. The story wasn't leaked by a nattily dressed anchor man with blow-dried hair.

My guess is that the restoration of Peter after his betrayal took more than the exchange reported in John 21:15-23. We may never know. It was too personal to be divulged even in the recording of Scripture. Our curiosity may lead us to long to know what Peter might have gotten off his chest in that encounter. What a guest he would have been on a talk show or the luncheon circuit! But that is part of intimacy with God.

Our mistake back there in college was that we didn't know what we were asking of Mel. We had not yet learned that intimacy means quality instead of quantity. Not built on the ecstasy of spiritual gymnastics, joyful intimacy with God is forged in a daily interaction with Scripture and prayerful obedience to what we read there. A lot of that joy will overflow into the lives of other people. It should. But some will be treasured privately, because to disclose it would cheapen and violate that joy.

Has God become "Abba," or Dad, to us? Christ died to make that kind of spiritual intimacy a reality. Our mouths know the word: intimacy. Ask Christ to show you the truth of it. It may seem awkward at first, but the song of His presence will gradually prove almost intoxicating. In the process, we may suffer some bruises and even some "broken bones." But out of the innermost part of us will begin to blossom the authentic openness and joy of a relationship that the world is waiting to see. That broken-down world has not only forgotten how to dance. It's a world that is rapidly giving up hope that there is any beautiful spiritual music to dance to.

NOTES:
1. From the study notes of *The NIV Study Bible* (Grand Rapids: The Zondervan Corporation, 1985), page 838.
2. Lanny Wolfe, "Whatever It Takes" (Lanny Wolfe Music Co., ASCAP, used by permission of the Benson Company).
3. Sinclair B. Ferguson, *Know Your Christian Life: A Theological Introduction* (Downers Grove, Illinois: InterVarsity Press, 1981), page 39.
4. Elizabeth Skoglund, *Coping* (Ventura, California: Regal Books, 1979), page 48.
5. See Romans 5:3-5, James 1:2-4, and 1 Peter 1:6-7.

CHAPTER SEVEN

Cardiac Renewal

Create in me a clean heart, O God,
And renew a steadfast spirit within me.
Do not cast me away from Thy presence,
And do not take Thy Holy Spirit from me.
Restore to me the joy of Thy salvation,
And sustain me with a willing spirit.
Psalm 51:10-12

Have you ever felt like you were trapped on something resembling an electric toy train, chugging monotonously in circles? On the surface, our lives look like they're going somewhere, but when we take another look, the scenery looks strangely familiar.

How is it that we can grow older in the Christian faith without necessarily growing stronger or deeper? We keep falling over the same things. There's a repetitiveness about our failings that gradually deepens into a rut. Even though we may realize it's happening, we grow so accustomed to life in the rut that we passively allow it to deepen into a lifestyle. Not only do we become stagnant, but we get to the point where we're actually eroding.

Many people become painfully aware of this catch-22 somewhere along the process. The awareness of lost spiritual assets can be a cruel presence that infects with a creeping paralysis. Frustration and defeat have been a way of life for so long that any hope of

79

rescue wheezed out its last breath long ago. The sense of futility seems to be sealed both without and within.

A girl in a discussion group once told me, "I just don't believe people really change." But this isn't the same as saying that people can't *be changed.* While you and I may be too weak to break out of holding patterns of sin that have held us back for years, God specializes in freeing people from their devastated past and rebuilding from that sinful rubble.

David was desperate. God's pardon was obviously not enough unless a radical change could be included.[1] The former without the latter is a local anesthetic that wears off quickly, leaving the individual to return to his previous infection with the sin disease. David saw that a pardon for sin alone was useless if he were left to fall back into the clutches of old passions and desires. What he really craved was a pure heart. Only God could give it. But God didn't have to be begged or badgered. He is a creator by nature. God doesn't create and recreate out of compulsion or obligation. He delights and excels in it. B. F. Lockeridge said, "He made everythin' from nothin' and hung it on empty space and told it to stay there."

David meant business. The intensity that shined through in his life has parallels in the New Testament and throughout church history. Caught in a restless agitation and deep dissatisfaction, David was a man set in steel, determined to pursue God's righteousness alone. He refused to be satisfied with the spiritual status quo.

David's number needs to increase. We need many more of his kind. Our problem isn't that the church is totally dead or that the world has completely infiltrated the church on all sides. The indictment against us is that we've become *comfortable* with lukewarm spirituality and compromise with the world. We've become so satisfied with mediocrity that any spirit of sacrifice that threatens our lifestyle of convenience quickly passes from our minds.

The quest for a new heart

Jesus' words in the Beatitudes don't strike us with the impact they must have made on His first hearers. He said, "Blessed are those who hunger and thirst for righteousness" (Matthew 5:6). Not many in Western industrial societies know much about hunger and thirst. To us, they're mild discomforts that can be quickly relieved by the turn of a faucet or a quick trip to the refrigerator. To Jesus' hearers, the words were nagging reminders of a creeping threat of death men would avoid at any cost.

A pastor from famine-stricken Sudan stood addressing a well-heeled American congregation. He stood trembling, with tears streaming down his cheeks, unable to speak at first. Finally he choked out, "You have no idea what it does to me to see you Americans waste water." A simple enough statement—but one with impact. Here was a man who rightly understood thirst.

The quest for a new heart is no idle pursuit. It may mean enduring in the face of sacrifice, disappointment, and misunderstanding. It absolutely means refusing to be satisfied with merely being pardoned without being changed. What does a new heart from God look like? David's words "restore" and "renew" show that something was missing in his life. Exactly what? This new heart has at least three components, which we will deal with one at a time.

A steadfast spirit

We live in a culture where "the gospel of whatever feels good" has infiltrated the church. Emotions often sway us more than we might realize. Certainly we should expect ups and downs in our Christian life. But none of us will ever live in constant gloom or ecstasy. Joy will surprise us and crises will plunge us into the depths. But we will spend most of our time walking across miles of flat country where the scenery doesn't change very much. It's land where fatigue of the soul deceives us by creeping up on us slowly.

After a huge redwood once fell in one of our national parks, researchers examined it and made some interesting discoveries. By analyzing the grain and rings of the wood as well as scars on the trunk, they learned that the tree had survived two hundred years of disasters. At least two landslides had almost buried it. Numerous fires and strikes by lightning also left their mark, but hadn't killed the majestic tree. What finally caused it to topple? Beetles gnawed it to death! Anxiety, fear, and the drag of the flesh likewise kill us with tiny bites, slowly but surely draining away the essence of our lives. In complete contrast, a steadfast, growing spirit that does not fluctuate with the circumstances is a rare treasure.

My heroes have changed through the years. Like most believers, I have admired those who have had great experiences or done great things for Christ. They still encourage me. But I've learned some things about Christian dedication. Many of those who "burn out for Jesus" aren't really driven by commitment but by compulsion. They're workaholics who just can't say no. Such people are undisciplined, operating without priorities. The emotional needs of their family members go unmet. They abuse their health, shaving years off the lives that God wants them to use wisely.

Now I admire Christians who last, who have staying power. Those select few who learn to walk a straight line day after day have earned my deepest respect and admiration. The spotlight rarely catches these folk, but they don't seem to mind. Thank God every church seems to have at least a few.

The steadfast spirit that enables us to walk the flat country of the heart, whether the skies are gray or clear, doesn't appear overnight. When God rebuilds a gutted life, He builds it up a brick at a time. Resilient endurance is the badge of people under construction. Some people resemble human pinballs, slammed passively from bumper to bumper. But the person with a steadfast spirit is actively willing to remain under pressure of any kind, as long as God wills, in order to grow stronger.

We . . . exult in our tribulations; knowing that tribulation brings about perseverance; and perseverance, proven character; and proven character, hope. (Romans 5:3-4)

Consider it all joy, my brethren, when you encounter various trials; knowing that the testing of your faith produces endurance. And let endurance have its perfect result, that you may be perfect and complete, lacking in nothing. (James 1:2-4)

Blessed is the person who wants growth so badly that he refuses to shrink from the process that produces it. David wanted grace that could not only weather fierce storms but also bring stability into a life tossed with guilt, regrets, and fear of discovery. Sin fractures our ability to last, to resist the beetles that chew on our lives through unending petty aggravations and mundane routine. Then, when the pressures intensify, the beams of our soul no longer stand the strain. We collapse. That's why David coveted a steadfast spirit more than gold.

The indwelling of the Holy Spirit

Operating from an Old Testament understanding of the Holy Spirit, it seemed to David that the gifts, grace, and guidance of the Spirit's presence were gone and could be lost for the remainder of his life. How could he keep from looking over his shoulder and fearing a repetition of the nightmare of the decline and fall of his predecessor, King Saul?

Have you ever witnessed the collapse of someone God has used in your life? Maybe a favorite pastor or even the one who led you to Christ. This person's spiritual demise would be both shocking and heartbreaking. David's shaky plea, asking that the Spirit not be stripped away from him, is a humbling reminder that not only can our heroes and mentors fall: so can we. When you and I see the poison that laid a spiritual giant like David in the dust loose in our own bloodstream, we become justifiably frightened. We are compelled to shout out, "Do not cast me from Your presence or take Your Holy Spirit from me." This is the frantic prayer of someone who realizes, "It's happening to *me!*"

We have more reason to shout out this prayer than David did. His understanding of the Spirit's work falls far short of what we know from the New Testament. There we find the work of the Holy Spirit described in far more depth and detail than what David could read in the early scrolls of God's Word. But greater knowledge means greater accountability. Perhaps we know more truth about the Spirit's working, but David might have known more about the reality of His power. In quiet moments, he felt the loss and grieved over the alienation and blindness covering him like a shroud. Sadly, we often do not. Many times we are so overconfident of the indwelling presence of the Spirit, which cannot be taken from true Christians, that we forget that the Holy Spirit can be held back by our failure to yield to His guidance.

A group of deacons met one night to discuss a problem in the church. Reaching an impasse, one of them suggested they spend some time praying, seeking the mind of the Holy Spirit. At this, the chairman bristled and said, "Holy Spirit, hell! *We* run this church!" Some, on hearing this anecdote, snicker at the thought of the chairman caught with egg on his face. But we should weep, because this very attitude, at least in spirit, has spread to almost every segment of the church. The individual attitude of the deacon chairman has mushroomed into a corporate mentality. "*We* run this church! And *I* run my life!"

Paul wasn't idly beating the breeze when he said, "Do not grieve the Holy Spirit of God, with whom you were sealed for the day of redemption" (Ephesians 4:30). He had simply been reading over David's shoulder. Every thought, action, and attitude should be sensitized and permeated with the Spirit's influence. When we squelch His influence through flagrant disobedience or sheer neglect, He is understandably grieved.

When we don't get our way, we often get angry, disgusted, and even pout. But projecting our attitudes in such a negative way is always a mistake. Although the Spirit may come in a whirlwind, He painfully steals away in a whisper. Oswald Sanders said it well: "The evidence is that He is regretfully compelled to withdraw His gracious influence and working, and His grief is reflected in the gloom and heaviness of the estranged heart."[2]

A willing spirit

I'm a history buff. Not many historical films, especially war movies, escape my attention. One evening World War II was being fought in front of my popcorn when a scene jumped right off the screen directly into my memory bank because it was both ridiculous and true. A German position was being shelled so heavily that the situation became hopeless. A white flag fluttered weakly. An officer and two soldiers walked into the clearing. The soldiers' uniforms were ripped to shreds and soiled bandages seemed to be the only thing holding them together. But (only in Hollywood!) the officer wore an immaculate suit, with sharp creases and polished buttons. Swaggering up to the Allied commander, he said, "We have come to negotiate the terms of surrender!" But the incredulous reply was right to the point: "You will surrender unconditionally, and here are the terms."

That's so much like us, isn't it? Modern man demands the right to dicker, barter, or negotiate with God, who demands unconditional surrender. David sought a willing, renewed spirit. Knowing that a guilty man has nothing to negotiate with, David longed for the kind of perpetual inner kneeling that would receive mercy gratefully and render obedience ungrudgingly.

Too many of us are trying to strike the best deal with God, when we should be willing to yield fully to Him. Our failure to show a willing spirit manifests itself in at least three ways.

First, we hide behind the word "simple." A lot of people claim to want a faith that is simple. The gospel, although profound, is indeed simple and uncomplicated. But by simple, many people mean something that can serve as an emotional security blanket that can be taken up or left behind at will. They want no part of a faith that requires unconditional obedience to any absolute Master or inconveniences them by demanding changes in their lifestyle.

Second, some of us are trying to bribe God with our mere presence or token service, determined to keep God at arm's length by insisting that church attendance (often sporadic) and financial giving (usually meager) are enough. This minimizing of our relationship with God reveals a mind-set that regards evangelism and discipleship as something just for clergy and other fanatics.

Third, some of us are zealous to know God's will, but only as one of many options. The willing spirit, on the contrary, is passionate to obey God regardless of the circumstances or outcome. Such an obedient attitude is the mark of real maturity and a prerequisite to knowing God's will. But we twist that around by wanting to know God's will just so we can evaluate it alongside our other options. We'll decide in favor of God's will as long as it serves our selfish ends better than the course we've already chosen. This is exactly why many Christians are restrained by self-inflicted mediocrity. Living as if we had authority and competence to weigh God's will in the balance by withholding obedience is sheer, arrogant sin.

We trust ourselves way too much. In almost any situation, we're very much inclined to suspect and judge the motives and actions of others, while leaving our own unexamined. We should keep our lopsided discernment at home. Doesn't Richard Foster strike a deep chord on this theme of spiritual humility?

> It is the ability to lay down the terrible burden of always needing to get our own way. The obsession to demand that things go the way we want them to go is one of the greatest bondages in human society today.[3]

The roots of power have been tragically mistaken. Spiritual power comes not with visibility, but with unseen depth; not with flash, but obedience. Needing to get our own way is deeply embedded in the cultural and religious status quo. We need to learn a lesson from the psalmist and king. David's desire for a willing spirit should serve as a tonic for our selfish age.

Steadfastness, the intimate presence of the Holy Spirit, and a willing spirit are worthy trophies. But the arena where these trophies are won is rarely in the spotlight.

My wife and I were once admiring some beautiful wall hangings. Upon closer examination, we found that these tapestries were made of the most intricate stitches. In stark contrast, public religious displays slapped together loosely with the right "holy talk" are utterly repulsive. That kind of life is a spiritual Frankenstein—death hideously passing itself off as life. A life that loves God, however, is made up of a million tiny stitches. These stitches are laid in place every time that life chooses to obey Christ in the tiniest thing or everyday circumstance.

A pure, renewed heart. People coming to Christ may have their own agendas, but He will settle for nothing less than a transformed life. Anyone wanting such spiritual cardiac renewal will never have his or her hopes dashed by Jesus Christ.

NOTES:
1. A. A. Anderson, *The Book of Psalms,* Volume 1, *The New Century Bible* (London: Oliphants, 1972), page 398.
2. J. Oswald Sanders, *The Holy Spirit and His Gifts* (Grand Rapids: Zondervan, 1981), page 96.
3. Richard Foster, *Celebration of Discipline* (San Francisco: Harper and Row, 1978), page 97.

CHAPTER EIGHT

Seek First His Kingdom, Not Your Own

Then I will teach transgressors Thy ways,
And sinners will be converted to Thee.
Psalm 51:13

■

In one of his essays, George Orwell described a wasp that "was sucking jam on my plate and I cut him in half. He paid no attention, merely went on with his meal, while a tiny stream of jam trickled out his severed esophagus. Only when he tried to fly away did he grasp the dreadful thing that had happened to him."

Orwell's account is a concise parable of many people in Western society—people too busy indulging their appetites and desires to realize that they have been severed from the very Source of life, and that thus they are dying.

One man sits in his designer hot tub nursing a second martini. He looks out past a Lincoln and a Mercedes in the driveway and a large swimming pool to the two acres of carefully manicured lawn. His mind runs down a catalog of toys: a yacht, a resort cabin, and every technological bauble imaginable. Having it all had been his goal, and have it he does. But during all this process of material acquisition, how did his wife and children become such strangers?

Another man sits watching the steam rising from the cup of coffee that will grow cold as he sits staring straight ahead. He had given everything he had to the company, and now this. The company called it early retirement. It was supposed to be some kind of a favor. But he sees himself forced out at an age of high productivity to make way for younger men paid lower salaries. Feelings of rejection and betrayal cut deep. What will he do now?

We don't talk often about needing a sense of purpose or meaning, but sometimes it just leaks out at odd times when our defenses are down. Maybe it's late at night or in a cut-rate philosophical conversation at someone's Christmas party. Indeed, our ideas on life and what makes it tick sound very impressive as we stand in little groups sloshing punch in Styrofoam cups. But among the many options available today, people find it increasingly difficult to find goals and objectives that will sustain the weight of everyday living and pass the acid test of dying.

In tune with God
Dostoevsky wrote, "Man's whole business is to prove that he is a man and not a cog-wheel. . . ." The quest for meaning and purpose prods and nags us all. That's why the "live-for-now" philosophy is a bedfellow with cold feet. As good and convenient as it sounds, none of us can outrun the notion that our life must count for something beyond tonight's sunset.

Marie Antoinette remarked, "Nothing tastes." Many of us know that sense of a heartbeat pounding furiously in a vacuum. For most people, this void is a deep undercurrent swirling darkly beneath the surface roar of our daily lives. For others who wrestle with depression, a voice rises from the depths to whisper through a sneer that life is a pointless practical joke. Is there no significance whatsoever to our existence? When someone like David discovers something that "tastes," we should indeed pay attention.

Emerging from empty affluence and still stinging from sin publicly rebuked, David discovered a sense of meaning that swallowed all other pursuits. The key to unlocking satisfying purpose and direction in life could be found in his choice of pronouns. David said, "I will teach transgressors *Thy* ways, and sinners will [turn back] to *Thee*." In narcissistic times like ours, when people see everything through the lenses of their own egos, David seems out of tune. But from God's viewpoint, he's not only in tune, but in broad harmony. David had learned that among all challengers, God alone was a sufficient master. The earthly king no longer needed to dazzle men with his own claims, but now longed for them to know the heavenly King whose grace had cleansed him.

Who masters you?

Part of the genius of Jesus' teaching was His ability to shake men free from their own egos. Jesus confronted His hearers one day with an idea that no man can have two masters (Matthew 6:24). His keen insight assumed that while no man can serve two masters, everyone was surely serving one. Whether or not an individual is mastered is not even an issue. It's a given. Jesus knew that the real issue is choosing our master deliberately and well, because that important choice will control and color every area of our lives.

Young families are tied to a mortgage. Executives are mesmerized by the top rung of the corporate ladder. The professional student never has enough schooling, so he buries mailmen with endless applications, transcripts, and catalogs in an endless pursuit of never-earned degrees. The discovery of authentic meaning and purpose in life does not depend on constantly finding bigger things that *we* can conquer. Ironically, it's quite the opposite. We must make sure that we're being mastered by the *right* thing.

What actually masters us? How can we tell? It's certainly hard to be objective. We're like a man trying to read a billboard from a distance of two inches. We're just too close.

For example, most of us pursue our life goals without ever

taking the time to think them through. We just keep dutifully pursuing them.

One of our astronauts had completed an important mission in outer space. At a point when there should have been strong feelings of accomplishment, the man suffered from deep, almost suicidal depression. He realized that everything he'd wanted his life to be had been reached, and there seemed to be no place to go. Our goals leave us hollow in even more barren, mundane ways: the man who longs for retirement only to be swamped with boredom, and the executive who finally gets that promotion only to want another.

The test of a worthy life goal lies in the wake of its achievement. What a shame to discover that, upon reaching a goal, the joy consisted solely in striving for it! A worthy goal, upon achievement, should give way to another. They should all be intermediate steps in a wider process. The letdown and emptiness that crashes into highly motivated lives reveals that these people were mastered by things that were too small and closed-ended. "Coming from" isn't enough. Men clamor for purpose, for always having a direction to "go to."

A look at noted scientists and great thinkers sheds interesting light on this subject. Although these men have made history and won the highest awards with their discoveries, few seem content to rest on their laurels. They are characterized by a restless urge to expand. But in this urge to expand, these people do not seem as much driven as drawn. Their striving doesn't resemble compulsion as much as it does the patient persistence of the visionary.

I know one of these men. He works as the director of the planetarium at a local college. Every month this man pulls together a fine show. One night we attended a show highlighting a number of planets visible in the sky that month. At the end of the program, the director offered to take everyone down to the observatory so that we could actually see the real thing through the telescope. Although the guy was sick with the flu, he stood there in the dark thoroughly enjoying our getting caught up in the same wonder that had captivated him. Is it possible to have a goal that reaches out from beyond limits, beyond space and time, drawing us and fulfilling us? Is it possible to have a sense of purpose and meaning, independent of circumstances and levels of achievement, that satisfies us completely?

The hint of the infinite in Christ's voice captured the attention of many people. The challenge of the limitless, the eternal, shone through His offer of living water (John 4:10-14), the bread of life (John 6:35), treasure in heaven (Matthew 19:21), and the call to be fishers of men (Matthew 4:19). In light of His words, how tragic that many Christians find themselves mastered by things so very small. Sometimes we're numb to it. We read the Bible, pray, attend church services, and serve in many ways, and yet, as with Marie Antoinette, nothing "tastes."

If God's people fail to find an overall principle for integrating every segment of life, they will find themselves fragmented over a host of secular and badly diluted Christian agendas. And that is exactly what has happened. Often leadership is to blame. In attempts to recruit volunteers or fill ministry slots, leaders and committees can become so preoccupied with getting the job done that candidates for ministry aren't challenged with the privilege and responsibility of being ambassadors for Christ. Manipulation, begging, or browbeating cheapens serving Christ until ministry is whittled down to a thankless, unfulfilling task that still must be done for some obscure reason.

Great tasks galvanize average people into greatness. In the early days of World War II, Germany quickly overran France. Overnight, French people found Nazis in the streets and their leaders in collaboration with their conquerers. Organized armed resistance had been crushed. Rather than live in defeat and captivity, common people all over France banded together against their enemy, and wrote a courageous little chapter of history called the French Resistance.

Average people took incredible risks in order to fight against a terrible evil. A little sewing circle of old ladies became the sharpest pickpockets and forgers in Paris as they worked to falsify documents of passage for anyone fleeing the Nazis. Shoe salesmen and gourmet chefs learned to handle explosives. Farmers became crack shots with confiscated weapons. College professors and students wrote, printed, and distributed leaflets to rally the grass roots. This struggle against the Nazi regime wasn't something done on the side. It demanded everything they had—and it transformed them in the process.

> We lived in the shadows as soldiers of the night but our lives were not dark and martial. We were young and we were gay. We loved and . . . we laughed perhaps more than we do today. There were arrests, torture, and death for so many of our friends and comrades, and tragedy awaited all of us just around the corner. But we did not live in or with tragedy. We were exhilarated by the challenge and rightness of our cause. It was in many ways the worst of times and in just as many ways the best of times, and the best is what we remember today.[1]

For Christians, the ultimate source of meaning that keeps us stretching beyond ourselves, beyond time itself, is the Kingdom of God. Jesus said, "Seek first [God's] kingdom, and His righteousness; and all these things shall be added to you" (Matthew 6:33). A Christian throwing the weight of his soul behind the Kingdom of God will find himself in a struggle that addresses his sin, marriage, children, friendships, career, hobbies, ambitions, failures, and discouragements. But that's not all. He will find himself engaging even broader concerns, such as world hunger, poverty, affluence, technology, education, medicine, pollution, the arts, the military, economics, politics, and a hundred other fields. Elton Trueblood wisely said:

The full commitment of millions of Germans, prior to and during the Great War, was to Adolf Hitler and his cause. Other millions are today committed to Marxism. Christians have no monopoly on commitment; they simply have a different object. A Christian is a person who confesses that, amidst the manifold and confusing voices heard in the world, there is one Voice which supremely wins his full assent, uniting all his powers, intellectual and emotional, into a single pattern of self-giving. That voice is Jesus Christ. . . . He believes in Him with all his heart and strength and mind. Christ appears to the Christian as the one stable point or fulcrum in all the relativities of history. Once the Christian has made this primary commitment he still has perplexities, but he begins to know the joy of being used for a mighty purpose by which his little life is dignified.[2]

David at last tapped into a stream of meaning flowing steadily far above the surface rush of his pressured existence as king. In the jaws of spiritual crisis, he learned what was important from God's perspective. Regardless of how his personal life and his nation's politics went from this point, David wanted to live so that others would come to know God.

The wonder that wraps itself around God's calling can grow dull and stale when we take our eyes off Him. People like David, however, never seem to get tired of turning it over and over in their hearts. And interestingly enough, this pondering of the call to serve in God's Kingdom has always been a wellspring of life bubbling up in even the driest of times. To have the wonder of being chosen, of being His, washed over us all our lives—this is enough. In fact, it is the ultimate satisfaction.

David's life was no longer rooted in wealth or power. He would eventually lose both. But in a restored relationship with God that moved him into the hearts and lives of others, David found meaning in life that refused to unravel when his erratic circumstances did.

We were made for more exquisite things than trying to fill empty days with our own thunder. But we must all choose. Will I go on tinkering on my own agenda and my own kingdom, which will pass away when I do? Or will I tie my life and destiny to His life, His cause, His Kingdom? Only Christ offers the calling whereby we can harness our lives to a source of purpose that lasts forever.

NOTES:
1. David F. Schoenbrum, *Soldiers of the Night* (New York: E. P. Dutton, 1980), page 489.
2. Elton Trueblood, *Company of the Committed* (New York: Harper & Row Publishers, 1961), page 23.

CHAPTER NINE

Your Brother's Keeper

Then I will teach transgressors Thy ways,
And sinners will be converted to Thee.
Psalm 51:13

One of the first American missionaries to Taiwan, a man named Oz, told me about his early days there. Fleeing the Communists, frightened Chinese people poured onto the island faster than adequate shelter could be built to house them. Shantytowns, with rickety huts made of whatever could be scrounged, sprang up everywhere.

One such town expanded until the front doors of some huts were only inches from a busy highway. Oz always hated driving this road for that very reason. He feared that a child would dart out in front of him. One day he was approaching the town and his heart sank as he saw a crowd gathered in the road ahead. Passing through the crowd, Oz saw a young boy lying in the road. Running at play from one of these makeshift huts, the boy had been hit by a truck and killed.

From behind him, Oz heard a terrible wailing, and turned to see a hysterical woman push through the crowd and throw herself on the lifeless body. She picked up the motionless boy and cradled him as if he were still her baby.

Oz ached to see this woman's pain, but nothing could have prepared him for what happened next. Looking down through her tears at the dead boy's face, she suddenly gave a strange smile of relief and joy. "Oh, it's all right," she said. "It's not mine." The woman literally dropped him in the road like a rock and walked away!

When Oz first told me about that woman, I was shocked and then outraged. But I've learned that my outrage was wasted. Why? Because I'm very much like her. As long as my personal world and concerns aren't touched, I can drop the pain of others rather quickly. As soon as that woman learned that the dead boy wasn't hers, neither was the pain. In fact, the dead boy ceased to be a genuine human being in her eyes. (Note the impersonal pronoun "it" that she used.) All of us, even though we may be Christians, fall into this kind of impersonal detachment all too easily. As long as the world's suffering millions are statistics without a face or a name, we can say with relief, "That's terrible, but they're not really mine."

Not only am I capable of this selfish kind of disinterest, but I've discovered even blacker thoughts banging around in my heart that I can't rationalize away. I truly hate prejudice and like to think that I'm relatively free of it. I have even fantasized that if I had lived back during the times of slavery, I would have been one of the enlightened ones. Caught up in this self-righteous reverie one day, I heard God speak quietly in my heart. "Dave," He said, "have you ever either told or laughed at a racial joke?" As a history buff, I've felt the heat of righteous indignation at the horrible details of Hitler's "final solution" for "the Jewish problem." My mind boggles at such poisonous hatred, and I wonder how human beings could be that way. Certainly I was above that. But then God brought other little incidents from my past to my attention, and I felt a deep sense of shame.

Most of us can probably recall personal times of falling prey to some form of chauvinism or prejudice. But no matter what shadowy guilt we may bear in this area, David's example can help us. Part of forgiveness for David meant seeing others of different backgrounds as being valuable to God. Maybe this was something restored to David from his previous perspective or perhaps it was something new implanted in his heart. In any event, David came out on the forgiven side of things with a concerned vision for the world. How desperately Western Christians need this kind of vision, we who get caught in cultural fog the second we pass the end of our own nose!

How broad is God's scope?

Who were the sinners and transgressors David was referring to in Psalm 51:13? Were they just the people he knew personally or saw daily in the street around the palace? It certainly included them. But remember that David was a king. Didn't his vocation also suggest that he would be able to personally influence dignitaries and officials from other lands? Couldn't a godly king making righteous foreign policy impact peoples not under his royal influence for the domain of God?

A vision for the world is not tied to someone's vocation. Christians aren't exempt from this kind of global view just because we don't happen to be Middle Eastern potentates or foreign ambassadors. David's worldwide view of things grew from the seed bed of knowing God, who is always concerned with the nations of the world.

> All the ends of the earth will remember and turn to the LORD, and all the families of the nations will worship before Thee. (Psalm 22:27)

> All nations whom Thou hast made shall come and worship before Thee, O Lord. (Psalm 86:9)

God's love and the scope of all He sees have never been restricted to certain individuals, to just Israel or the church. Scripture shouts this out from Genesis to Revelation. In the marvelous promise to Abraham (Genesis 12:1-3), we see that people throughout all the world would be blessed through this man's descendants. To Moses and Israel in the wilderness, God hinted that His choosing and using them was for something on a broader scale than just themselves (Exodus 19:5-6, Numbers 14:21). Psalmists and others who worshiped God recognized that He was worthy of praise and desired not just the praise of Israel but the praise of all nations (Psalm 72:8-11).

The prophets were visionary men, gifted by God to see across the ages. None of them could surpass Isaiah for breadth and depth of vision (Isaiah 42:1-7, 49:1-12). Joel (Joel 2:28-29) and Micah (Micah 4:1-4) likewise had a sense of the scope of God's burning love for all the world. After the breaking of the great silence of God that began at the death of Malachi, the awareness of God's love for the entire world was woven into the very fabric of the faith of "ordinary" men like Simeon (Luke 2:25-32).

This degree of passion and concern for all nations can be observed in the life of Jesus. Sometimes it peppered His conversation while He was teaching on other things (Mark 13:9-10). It also rang loud and clear as some of the most important of His last words.

> "All authority has been given to Me in heaven and on earth. Go therefore and make disciples of all the nations, baptizing them in the name of the Father and the Son and the Holy Spirit, teaching them to observe all that I commanded you; and lo, I am with you always, even to the end of the age." (Matthew 28:18-20)

> "You shall receive power when the Holy Spirit has come upon you; and you shall be My witnesses both in Jerusa-

lem, and in all Judea and Samaria, and even to the remotest part of the earth." (Acts 1:8)

The early church and its leaders picked up this theme. That great church at Antioch, planted with believers who were fleeing persecution in Jerusalem, was a great model. One day in Antioch, some people went a little crazy and did the unthinkable: they started telling Gentiles about Jesus (Acts 11:19-21). The ethnic background of a person meant nothing to them. What a mixed bag of spiritual mongrels and half-breeds their leadership was! (Acts 13:1). All that was necessary was that you loved Jesus because your sins were forgiven.

God loved these outsiders so much that He went to great lengths to convince the most hardheaded leader of the church, Peter, that these Gentiles were proper targets of evangelism (Acts 10). Then God handpicked the man He would use to spearhead the thrust of the gospel across Asia and into Europe: Saul of Tarsus (Acts 9:1-16).

Their torch and their task of world vision have been passed down to us, and even beyond. At the very end of the Bible, we see that the book of Revelation refers to an extraordinary time in the future when God's deep love for all nations will no longer be unreciprocated.

And the city has no need of the sun or of the moon to shine upon it, for the glory of God has illumined it, and its lamp is the Lamb. And the nations shall walk by its light, and the kings of the earth shall bring their glory into it. (Revelation 21:23-24)

And on either side of the river was the tree of life, bearing twelve kinds of fruit, yielding its fruit every month; and the leaves of the tree were for the healing of the nations. (Revelation 22:2)

Characteristics of a break-out

Copernicus was a great scientist. But if we could talk to the man in the street of that day, we would soon discover that most people thought him to be a firstrate heretic. Copernicus discovered that the sun was the center of the solar system with the planets revolving around it. The notion that we simply weren't at the center of things anymore made people angry.

If Christians are to have an impact for God's Kingdom, many of us need a Copernican kind of "break-out," where we are willing to face the facts and stop being the center and sum of all things. But we in the church had better get moving in our global perspective because we have to catch up to a world whose view is already global. In economics, politics, and military affairs, no nation on earth is an island doing as it pleases.

Rich sheiks in the Middle East make decisions behind closed doors that lead to American motorists lining up for miles at the gas pumps. Brazilian workers who work for low wages start a domino effect that results in layoffs at a tractor plant in Iowa. International terrorists and fanatical despots who once would have been instantly crushed are now handled with kid gloves. Political alliances and trade agreements complicate things until small nations can hold much larger, more powerful nations at bay.

Western Christians need a global view. For one thing, our inflated pride in being the hub of Christendom needs to undergo a deflation process. In Africa, South America, China, Korea, and other parts of Asia, the church is growing at an astounding rate, in many places faster than the population. Countries that are far below our standard of living have growing churches with an on-fire spirituality that puts us to shame. And they are developing their own seminaries and mission boards. Leadership is emerging. Voices talking about the demise of Christianity in the West may not be as premature and pessimistic as we think. But at the same time, other parts of the world are experiencing the powerful movement of God's Spirit.

As we struggle to break out of this holding pattern, what can we look for as indicators that our vision out beyond the end of our nose is clearing up? Many things stand out. The first is the dream.

A dream that won't let you go

Many adults devalue imagination, thinking that it's something just for children. But we all have dreams. The problem is that we just don't talk about them. Too often we hide them away until they quietly and sadly die. But God won't let that happen. When the most common Christian begins to see the world through God's eyes, God gives birth to a dream of how that person can play a significant part in His Kingdom.

A dream from God almost defies our comprehension. That is, it may seem impossible for a hundred reasons, and yet it still refuses to die. A God-given dream requires grace. God never calls people to do things that they can do without Him.

A friend of mine has a dream. He's an excellent all-round handyman with considerable experience in electricity and construction. Both he and his wife care deeply for people in need. He would like to open a center where people who have no skills could come and be trained at little or no cost. They would also like to offer free classes on filling out job applications or social service forms, on literacy, and on English as a second language. This would be in addition to food and clothing distribution, as well as a medical clinic. And all this would be combined with a witness for Christ. Right now there are a thousand reasons (mostly financial) why this will never happen. Only God could pull it off. But the dream refuses to let them go.

And what about you? Your dream should raise important questions in your mind. How will this dream stretch you to trust God in a greater way? Will it galvanize other Christians into a living force for God's Kingdom? Will it reveal Christ to lost men? Will it help to reverse the fragmentation sin has caused at every level of human existence?

The cost of Christian growth

Sacrifice is the second indicator that we're breaking out of the rut. Be honest. How many Christians do you know whose Christianity has cost them very much? It stands to our deep shame that in the lives of most Western Christians the great sacrifices are reserved for the secular arenas of our lives. The great sacrifices many Christians are making are for their own pursuits and pleasures. People complain about being strapped, but there always seems to be enough money and time for nice vacations and season tickets for the local college or pro team. Even if we have to forgo eating out twice a month, cut out more expensive cuts of meat, and brutalize the budget, it will be worth it all when we finally get that deck with a hot tub on the back of the house, won't it?

Where are the comparable sacrifices in the spiritual dimension of our lives? We uproot the family and move hundreds of miles in order to climb the next rung of the corporate ladder. The opportunity looked good and the door seemed open. But was God ever asked? Or were we too busy packing to hear if He said no?

Ambition sees every open door, but is usually blind when it comes to discerning whose hand is on the latch. That's why I appreciate Greg. He was a graduate student at the university dental school where I was having some work done. We had some great fellowship under the shadow of his high-speed drill.

As graduation approached, Greg faced the big decision of where to begin his practice. There were opportunities on the West Coast and also only a few miles from the university. But he finally bought into a practice right there in town—a graveyard for guys just starting out.

Why did he do it? There was far more money in other places. But Greg belongs to a strong church in town where he teaches and serves as an elder. As a Christian, he believed that seeing his life invested for the Kingdom was more important than career advancement. Couldn't he have taught on the West Coast? Yes, but it wasn't Greg's choice to make—not when Jesus is Lord.

Many of us take considerable pains to prepare for retirement. But with all the trouble taken to decide what our income will be, where we'll live, and what we'll do, Christ is often sadly left out. In retirement, there is much time and vitality freed up that could be put to use for Jesus Christ. But how often is that factor even a consideration?

Christian growth costs in ultimate figures. Some tough questions must be stared down if we want to mature *God's* way rather than our own. What will it take to solidify your spiritual disciplines? How can you sharpen your spiritual gifts? Will it mean going to school or taking up correspondence study? Are you prepared to view aggravation and pain, both past and present, as finishing tools? What legitimate pursuits and pleasures may have to be forgone in making any of the above happen? Are you willing to work to maintain primary relationships (God, spouse, kids) during all this?

Borrowing pain

An important part of this process of breaking out of our tunnel vision takes me back to the little boy lying dead in the road. We must be willing to embrace the pain of other people—complete strangers—and I don't do that well. For one thing, pain isn't one of my favorite things. For another, I have plenty of my own without borrowing it. And third, I've seen enough of other people's problems to have more than a touch of the cynic in me.

I click on the television and there's one of those starving African kids with a bloated belly and flies swarming on his lips. Switching over to the news, I see five people lying in their own blood in the streets of Beirut. I click to Jacques Cousteau. He's always safe. This night's show is about cocaine traffic on the Amazon River. A pregnant young woman is caught smuggling drugs and both she and her four-year-old daughter are put in jail. Her baby will be born in prison. I live in a nice house, but God will never allow me to hide even there from people He weeps over.

Part of the underground

The voice on the phone was urgent. "Would you help me pull a surprise party on my husband?" she said. I jumped at the chance. Not only do I love a good conspiracy but her husband did, too, and had nailed me a number of times. So together we fixed the old boy.

Christians everywhere are part of a great conspiracy. In a series of addresses, Ralph Winter pointed out that all of Scripture is a chronicle of how God redeems sinful men to fight against the evil darkness that has usurped His world. Borrowing from the title of a popular science fiction movie, he named his series "The Kingdom Strikes Back."[1]

In terms of sheer numbers, Christians are a minority in the world today. Even if we live in an area where our faith is in the majority, we still live all of our lives on enemy soil. Third world countries may understand this better than we do. Pressure to compromise or to remain silent may be religious, political, economic, or relational in nature. It may be subtle or direct. But it's always present. Every Christian should see his life as his place on the front lines, where he has been stationed to fight a battle handed to him across the ages and to fight it well. Paul passed this mind-set along to Timothy:

> Suffer hardship with me, as a good soldier of Christ Jesus. No soldier in active service entangles himself in the affairs of everyday life, so that he may please the one who enlisted him as a soldier. (2 Timothy 2:3-4)

Every area of a Christian's life, every thought and action, must be evaluated in light of whether it helps or hinders us in fighting for God's Kingdom. It includes our spare time, the substance of our daydreams, professional advancement, and our relationships with other people.

An old classmate of mine was a medic in Vietnam. He

described to me how needless many of the casualties were. At night in combat zones, no lights were to be lit. But inevitably one soldier or another just had to have a cigarette. They knew the situation, the orders, and the risks, but surely the brief light of a match wouldn't make much difference. The light lasted only a second or two—just long enough for a sniper with an infrared scope to put a bullet through the soldier's temple. Anything that interferes with our fighting for the Kingdom, no matter how innocuous or respectable it may seem, must go.

Things we forget
In the daily rush of living and pain of unexpected crises, our sense of a global vision and the spiritual conflict gets dulled easily. Important things slip past us, things that we need to retain if we're to hold our cutting edge. First, God calls *all* Christians to be part of this larger spiritual picture. Somehow we've gotten the impression that God calls only young people, those who have major life-shaping decisions in front of them. But when Jesus was launching this worldwide venture called the church, did He phone the placement offices at the University of Judea and Jerusalem College to line up appointments with their top graduates? No, He called men with vested business interests, whose careers were well under way (Peter, Andrew, James, John, Matthew) and said, "Follow Me." He still does. No one is exempt by virtue of age or career status from being used by God.

Next, a soldier in combat takes orders, he doesn't give them. Too many Christians afford themselves the luxury of disobedience. They consider it enough to have sound doctrine or to have had some tremendous experience. Humble obedience to what the Bible says seems a bit laborious. When Jesus sent out the Twelve on their own for a brief plunge into ministry, He didn't give them gold cards, promise luxury suites at the Radisson, and tell them to rally at His condo by the Sea of Galilee. The disciples were sent traveling light and under strict orders into enemy territory to wage spiritual warfare—healing the sick, casting out demons, preaching the Kingdom of God. The call is still the same for us, whether the surroundings look like it or not.

Third, every Christian and every church is important. No one is insignificant by virtue of being too small. How sad and, in some cases, how infuriating to see Christians caught up in the spirit of the age so much that they can see God only in something really big. Countless churches have deep inferiority complexes because they can't measure up to larger congregations. But if these less-gargantuan churches could gather the people they've ministered to over the years, they would probably fill the place to the rafters.

One example is a small church in Sandy Creek, North Carolina. Their current membership stands at 130, with a Sunday school enrollment of 106. This church was the beginning of what is known today as the Southern Baptist Convention. Begun in 1755, it continues to this day, sharing Christ in its community and beyond.

At times this church was large, but through most of its history, it's been rather small. Yet small does not describe their impact. In the first seventeen years alone, this church planted 42 churches and ordained 125 pastors. Beyond that, it is impossible to calculate the extent of the ripple effect of its ministry. "It is the mother church, nay a grand-mother and a great grandmother of all the Separate Baptists in North Carolina eastward to the sea, westward toward the great river Mississippi; northward to Virginia and southward to South Carolina and Georgia."[2]

Size has little to do with spiritual impact. Some small churches hum with vitality, growing at least a measure, while some larger churches are nothing more than ornate mausoleums where the dead sit upright. Cemeteries grow, too.

Of course the reverse can be true as well. But every Christian is meant to have a sustained, significant impact for the Kingdom of God. Matters of prominence or obscurity are best left to Him.

I encountered a man through a newsletter who embodies this

humble world-consciousness. He lives in the city of Lhasa, Tibet, and has a simple two-room apartment on the local campus where he teaches. Missions personnel from America paid him a visit, and here's their report.

> He said, "I know of only one Tibetan Christian in this city of 200,000 people. God has given me a ministry of fasting and praying against the powers of darkness, and I have the witness in my own spirit that God is going to have victory in this country in the days and years ahead." We treated him to a Chinese meal in the hotel, and he said, "This is the best meal I've had in a year." We gave him some granola bars, some chocolates, a *Time* magazine and a shortwave radio. You can't imagine the delight of that dear man. Pray for him. He has committed himself to at least another year teaching English and agonizing before the Lord on behalf of the more than two million Tibetans. Probably less than half of one percent have ever heard the name of Jesus.[3]

This man has made a statement with his entire life that he *is* his brother's keeper, that the anonymous child lying in the road is his concern. He is also my concern, my responsibility. God cares about him. And God's cares should be my cares.

This man over in Tibet makes me feel shabby in spite of and perhaps because of my comparative abundance. He makes me feel shallow despite my theological education, and selfishly near-sighted in spite of some cherished notions of my adult sophistication. But something deep inside of me yearns to be like him, even if I never leave Iowa. Have you ever had that kind of feeling?

NOTES:
1. Ralph Winter, "The Kingdom Strikes Back: A New Perspective of the Church's Mission from Abraham to Christ's Coming" (Minneapolis: Dimension Tapes, Bethany Fellowship, 1982).

2. *Sandy Creek Baptist Church* (a pamphlet published by the Sandy Creek Baptist Church and Randolph Baptist Association).
3. *International Intercessors* (a prayer newsletter from World Vision International, Pasadena, California).

CHAPTER TEN

How Does His Kingdom Grow?

Then I will teach transgressors Thy ways,
And sinners will be converted to Thee.
Psalm 51:13

Churches are fortunate that their mailmen don't sue them. If our church is typical, the sheer poundage of religious junk mail we receive provides these postal employees with a viable substitute for a health club. Most of this religious material is selling something: films, seminars, fund-raising programs, tapes, or T-shirts.

But what they're really selling is growth, and that pushes my button. I do want my church to grow. But is church growth something that can be merchandised? Can our problems and the paralysis in the church be overcome by something as basic as making the right purchase?

Churches grow by spreading the gospel. That's the key. Evangelism must take place. The good news of Jesus Christ must be shared. It must be told. Good Christian lives are not enough. The gospel is content that can't be absorbed from the air the way a frog breathes through its skin. Sooner or later somebody must *say* something. No one has ever lived a life that reflected the nature

111

and purpose of God more than Jesus Christ, and He was far from silent. We must have the courage to speak out Who we belong to and why, for we are speaking to a world full of dying men.

The best way to help Christians do this, I'm told, is to train them. My denominational mail tells me how important this training is. And they have an assortment of programs that can be tailored to any church. And I agree with my mail. Training is important. This "equipping the saints" that Christians are hearing so much about isn't something dreamed up by the promotional department or an ad agency. It's a biblical task (Ephesians 4:11-12). But what about the thousands of people who have been trained, indeed, who have taken every evangelism training opportunity that has come along, yet still are not sharing their faith?

David can help. And many people need his help, because they're beginning to believe that this part of their walk with Christ just isn't going to come together. David doesn't offer another three-ring binder crammed with notes to people who already have at least one. Our training must start with motivation, not just content. When you've been where David has been, the truth about God's forgiveness doesn't have to be yanked from your throat like tonsils. It explodes. Here David gives us necessary reminders, focuses our aim, and puts the spur to our motives.

That dirty word
David reminds us first of all about who we're dealing with: sinners. Sin is a loaded word, almost a theological obscenity today. People are very conscious of self-esteem. They spend considerable time and energy mulling it over, brooding about it. Guilt is something they try to avoid at all costs. Many Christians have picked up the refrain that the only real sin is failing to feel good about yourself. Guilt is a low-volume commodity on the current spiritual market. But the scriptural fact is that part of the effect of the Holy Spirit's coming was that He would convince men of their sin (John 16:8-9).

Dr. Paul Brand, the world's foremost authority on leprosy, has said, "Thank God for inventing pain! I don't think He could have done a better job. It's beautiful."[1] While his sentiments sound strange to our ears, guilt is to the spirit what pain is to the body: a warning signal that something is vitally wrong. People must see they are terminally ill, spiritually speaking, to be drawn to the Cross. All manner of cheap lures abound (material prosperity, happiness, etc.), but if people are to find the cure—Jesus Christ—we must be willing to discuss it, even if we're branded as fanatics or made to feel unpopular.

Isn't there a "plan B"?
In every age and society, something about the gospel makes it offensive to the world around us. Today the exclusiveness of the gospel really puts a burr under many who listen to us. "Are you trying to tell me that the only way to God is through Jesus Christ?" they ask. That's exactly what Christianity is saying. That's what it's always said. Jesus taught it, and the apostles preached the same message.

> Jesus said to him, "I am the way, and the truth, and the life; no one comes to the Father, but through Me." (John 14:6)

> There is salvation in no one else; for there is no other name under heaven that has been given among men, by which we must be saved. (Acts 4:12)

Western society has cultivated some pretty exotic tastes in spirituality. Our society pays lip service to freedom of religion—as long as all the options remain open. We bristle at the thought of being told that we can't choose. God is Someone to believe in—as long as we reserve the right to dress and package Him any way we like. Tolerance and broad-mindedness are fruits of the spirit of this age.

We must hold the line with David and talk to sinners about sin, not about better karma or higher planes of reality. David sought to lead men to God—the *only* God, not the gods of the Philistines, the Moabites, the Moonies, or the New Agers. There is no "plan B." Sin is an equal opportunity strangler of the souls of men of all nations, races, and creeds. Satan knows the sin weakness of each one of us and has a lure to appeal to every weakness. Thus each person must find the Cross of Christ, or else perish. Such urgency pushes us to tell the truth even if we may not do it well. Consider the following case in point:

> When I was serving a little church in rural Georgia, a relative of one of my members died, and my wife and I went to the funeral as a show of support for the family. It was held in a small, hot, crowded, independent Baptist country church. They wheeled the coffin in and the preacher began to preach. He shouted, fumed, flailed his arms.
>
> "It's too late for Joe," he screamed. "He might have wanted to do this or that in life, but it's too late for him now. He's dead. It's all over for him. He might have wanted to straighten his life out, but he can't now. It's over."
>
> What a comfort this must be to the family, I thought.
>
> "But it ain't too late for you! People drop dead every day. So why wait? Now is the day for decision. Now is the time to make your life count for something. Give your life to Jesus!"
>
> It was the worst thing I had ever heard. "Can you imagine a preacher doing that kind of thing to a grieving family?" I asked my wife on the way home. "I've never heard anything so manipulative, cheap and inappropriate. I would never preach a sermon like that."
>
> She agreed with me that it was tacky, manipulative, callous. "Of course," she added, "the worst part of all is that it was true."[2]

Redeemed, and living like it

In telling people about God, David had drawn a bead on what would result. He said, "Sinners will be converted to Thee." Conversion implies a change—a real one.

A factory near my hometown had been sitting vacant. The former owners removed all their equipment, leaving the buildings sitting there empty. Vandals smashed most of the windows. Then a new firm purchased the site and renovated everything—new equipment, new wiring, massive repairs. Not only did the plant have a new facelift; it had a new product. Conversion means a new master, a new lifestyle, new values. It does not mean that we have a license to go through the motions of a decision for Christ only to return to our old way of life. If we're truly redeemed, then the logical thing to do is to live like it.

> Consider yourselves to be dead to sin, but alive to God in Christ Jesus. Therefore do not let sin reign in your mortal body that you should obey its lusts, and do not go on presenting the members of your body to sin as instruments of unrighteousness; but present yourselves to God as those alive from the dead, and your members as instruments of righteousness to God. (Romans 6:11-13)

> If any man is in Christ, he is a new creature; the old things passed away; behold, new things have come. (2 Corinthians 5:17)

While the second passage here talks about our new standing in Christ, it's a new standing that frees us to actually live differently.

Churches have become organizations instead of the organisms God intended. Too often we're viewed as the equivalent of an Elks Club for those who happen to have a religious bent. It's easy to join. Go through a class. Sign a card. Say some things that have been routinely memorized. Raise a hand. Walk an aisle.

But Jesus never put His finger on any of these as the means of entrance into His church. As He told Nicodemus, it requires a total spiritual rebirth into a new life (John 3:3-5). When the dust settled at Pentecost, the Spirit hadn't forged just another civic group, but the *church*—a temple made up of living stones. Coming to Christ and His church means putting our lives under the control of a new master and then living it out in the company of a community of others who have done the same.

Through the silence barrier

How do we break the ice even after we've been trained about what to say? It's not just the fear of ignorance or embarrassment that stops us in our tracks. But exactly what motivations should nudge us past the easy silence we fall so naturally into? At least three must have pressed themselves upon David.

One is *the fear of God.* A major intimidator of many is the fear of men, that is, fear of losing the good opinion of others or of someone getting angry with us. While this fear of people shouldn't cause us to back off, it still does. But who is easier to face: man or God? (Our answer to this question says a lot about how well we know both man and God.)

If someone developed a cure for a terminal disease and refused to share it, we would think him to be morally bankrupt, in spite of his achievement. How could David keep quiet about the forgiveness shown him, even though it meant bringing his sin out into the open? Not all motivation for evangelism is fully positive. Being honest about the gospel includes the accountability of those who understand its full orb. When asked about what kept him going on as a Christian, a friend replied, "I feel that hot breath on my neck." Paul felt it, too:

> We must all appear before the judgment-seat of Christ, that each one may be recompensed for his deeds in the body, according to what he has done, whether good or bad.

Therefore knowing the fear of the Lord, we persuade men, but we are made manifest to God; and I hope that we are made manifest also in your consciences. (2 Corinthians 5:10-11)

One day my wife and I were talking about growing old. She asked, "We'll never really retire, will we?" I said, "In terms of being completely inactive for God's Kingdom, probably not. We know too much."

A second motivation that should compel us to speak out is *compassion*. David really wanted sinners to be converted. It takes one to know one. Many Christians have aborted witnessing attempts for two reasons. First, they concentrate so intently on following every step of a memorized presentation that they fail to relate to the other person as an individual.

Cary Grant once spent an afternoon with a reporter who had planned a lengthy interview with the famous actor. Afterward, the reporter's friends peppered him with questions about what Mr. Grant was like. His answer might surprise you. "I spent the afternoon," he said, "with someone who made me feel I was the most important person in the world just by the way he looked at me." We desperately need the kind of compassion that people can see in our eyes and body language, as well as in our words.

The second reason we blow our opportunities with some people is that we knock ourselves out to win a theological argument at all costs. Some of us cannot allow ourselves to be shown up. But people only need to know that Jesus is the truth; they don't have to be convinced that we are right.

One winter day I drove my family to O'Hare Field in Chicago. They were going to North Carolina for a few days to stay with my wife's family. I was not in a good mood. A blizzard had almost closed both the expressway and the airport, and I didn't relish the idea of driving back through what I'd already seen. The prospect of going back to spend the next few days alone in an empty apartment didn't thrill me. I was also very tired, since I was working two full-time jobs at the time, putting in eighty hours a week.

As I was walking back through one of the concourses, I entered the main terminal on the way to my car. Suddenly a girl walked up and said, "Hello, sir, can I sell you a flower for your coat? All the handsome young men are wearing one today." I recognized right away that she was a devotee of Krishna. Ready for a spiritual battle, I told her that since I was a Christian, I couldn't buy one of her flowers and support her group. She said, "If you're a Christian, you know that Krishna and Christ are the same." Boy, was I ready with an argument that would put this girl away! But she was gone—gone so fast I couldn't even see where she disappeared to.

I realize now that the Lord, not Krishna, moved her out of there. As I drove north on a snow-swept freeway, He said to me, "Dave, if you can't witness about Me with the same love for people that I have for them, then I'd rather you just not do it." He was right. I didn't want that girl to find the riches of Christ. I wanted to win—to put a spread of four torpedoes in her at the waterline, and then watch her sink with a hiss and a giant bursting bubble. But knowing God's truth doesn't give us the license to start gunning down Krishnas or Moonies in airports.

One preacher summed up redemption this way: "God wants back what's His." Having been convicted, shattered, and restored, how could David not want for others what he'd been given? How could he watch others stumble through the same sin-induced blindness he had felt without being moved? Wouldn't he want to spare others some of the pain he'd been through if he could? How could David be silent? As we try to answer these same questions for ourselves, how can *we* be silent?

Jesus radiated total compassion. No one seems to have highlighted it better than Luke. If Luke's Gospel has a theme, it must be found in Luke 19:10: "The Son of Man has come to seek and to save that which was lost." The book bristles with parables about lost sheep (15:4-7), a lost coin (15:8-10), a lost son (15:11-32), and a good Samaritan (10:25-37).

Luke recorded fully Jesus' tenderness of heart toward hurting people: the raising of a widow's son (7:11-17), the healing of a crippled woman on the Sabbath (13:10-21), His encounter with Zacchaeus (19:1-27), and His encounter with the sinful woman at Peter's house (7:36-50). Luke alone tells of the painful rebuke Jesus gave the disciples when they took it upon themselves to judge the lost instead of loving them (9:51-56). And finally, only Luke shows Jesus weeping and lamenting over the lost city of Jerusalem (19:41-44).

This urgent longing for sin-wasted people to know God's forgiveness was contagious. Jesus spread it among His followers. Paul had it, too:

> Having thus a fond affection for you, we were well pleased to impart to you not only the gospel but also our own lives, because you had become very dear to us. (1 Thessalonians 2:8)

People will have an open ear—not when our arguments crush theirs, but when they know that we love them.

A third motivation for us to speak forth the gospel message is *joy.* Good news has to be shared. How could David have all the riches mentioned in this psalm restored to him and keep quiet? While the New Testament commands the church to evangelize, it doesn't do so in a negative, critical way. The early Christians never seemed to think of anything else to do with their faith but to give it away. It was the natural overflow of loving Jesus.

> These men did not spread their message because it was advisable for them to do so, nor because it was the socially responsible thing for them to do. . . . They did it because of

the overwhelming experience of the love of God which they had received through Jesus Christ. The discovery that the ultimate force in the universe was Love . . . had an effect on those who believed it which nothing could remove.[3]

Love is best expressed in joy.

Conversion and joy are closely related in the Acts of the Apostles, and it remained a characteristic thing about the early Christians which attracted others into their company. Their new faith did not make them miserable. Often outward circumstances were unpleasant enough, but that could not rob them of the joy which was their Christian birthright.[4]

A missionary in Lebanon echoes the same idea in telling about evangelism there. She says, "The people in the church don't have the dead eyes of people in the world." Witnessing is done with the same kind of joy one would have when announcing wedding plans or some other good fortune.[5]

An elderly teacher once told me about his experience teaching in an old country school in rural Arkansas. It was a one-room school where kids of all ages were lumped together. Time had dulled many of his memories, but he would never forget Arlie. Arlie's family lived way out in the hills and they were poor as dirt.

Arlie and Tommy would eat lunch together every day. Tommy's father owned the general store, which made them one of the richer families around. Nowhere was the gap between these two boys more evident than when they ate together. Arlie brought the same thing every day: flour biscuits covered with pork rind gravy, long grown cold. Tommy always had something different.

As Christmas approached, Tommy started bringing large navel oranges his father put in holiday fruit baskets. Arlie had never seen one—or tasted one. He sat fascinated as he watched

Tommy peel it. Tommy felt Arlie's eyes fasten on him, and asked if Arlie would like some. After all, they were friends, weren't they? So Tommy let Arlie eat the peels.

Day after day this went on. The teacher stood by the window every day at noon watching Arlie chew and swallow those bitter orange rinds as if they were the greatest thing in the world. "Please," the teacher silently pleaded. "Just let him have one real slice—just one." But it never happened.

Then the teacher made the decision to take things into his own hands. On the last day of school before Christmas vacation, he went to the store and bought a sack full of candy, small toys, and fruit, especially oranges.

The way to Arlie's house couldn't be traveled by car. Snow was starting to fall as the teacher parked his Model-T car by the railroad tracks and started walking the ties. All he could think of was getting this bag to the boy's house. After a while, the teacher could make out the path that cut through the woods to Arlie's. Light was fading fast. That was why he didn't see the root that snagged his boot and caused him to trip and spill his load in the path. Fumbling around in the dark in the fresh snow, he gathered up what he could, stuffed it into the wet sack, and went on.

Arlie sure was surprised to see his teacher at the door. And his eyes were wide and bright when the bag was dumped on the table. Immediately he grabbed an orange and tore off a chunk of the peel. Before the boy could get the peel to his mouth, the teacher took Arlie's hand and said, "Wait! Stop! It's like this." And with that the teacher took the orange and peeled it. As he did, the room filled with the fragrance of the fruit. Everyone in the room was in awe.

Then the teacher broke the orange in two and all the children "oohed" over the misting juice spraying in the air. Tearing off a single slice, the teacher turned to Arlie and said, "Here." As he told me about this years later, the teacher said, "I will never forget looking into Arlie's eyes when he bit down and the juice and the flavor of that orange exploded on his tongue. It was the look of a boy who never in his wildest dreams could imagine that God could make something that would taste so good."

"O taste and see that the LORD is good," said the young psalmist David (Psalm 34:8). Telling others the good news of the Savior is difficult for many of us. But we forget too easily that God has already done the truly hard part. He gave His Son to become a man and to die a hideous, undeserved death for the sins of all other men. He sent the Holy Spirit to convict men of their sin and to reveal Jesus Christ as the Savior they need. Finally, God even instills faith in the hearts of men to believe in that Savior.

All that God leaves for us is the joyous part, the part that was left to the teacher of a small boy in rural Arkansas. To a world that in a million different ways is cramming its belly with bitter peelings and thinking it to be pretty good stuff, God sends you and me with that first bite of something far richer than anything those people have ever dreamed of. Why would we ever keep it to ourselves?

NOTES:
1. Philip Yancey, *Where Is God When It Hurts?* (Grand Rapids: Zondervan, 1977), page 23.
2. William H. Willimon, "Advent Meditation," *Christian Century* (December 3, 1986), page 1086.
3. Michael Green, *Evangelism in the Early Church* (Grand Rapids: Eerdmans, 1970), page 236.
4. Green, *Evangelism,* pages 185-186.
5. "Perseverance in Lebanon Brings Credibility," *Word and Way: Journal of the Missouri Baptist Convention* (November 13, 1986), page 12.

CHAPTER ELEVEN

An Audience of One

Deliver me from bloodguiltiness, O God, Thou God of my salvation;
Then my tongue will joyfully sing of Thy righteousness.
O LORD, open my lips,
That my mouth may declare Thy praise.
Psalm 51:14-15

Cameras snap and whir. Cars from at least six states line up at the curb and tour buses roll through this sleepy little town on a regular basis. What's the attraction? A religious shrine is the focal point of the community and a tourist stop in the area. Although the structure is rough, there is a grotesque beauty in its composite construction of gold, sea shells, old bottles, and polished semi-precious stones.

The remarks visitors make while strolling the grounds are interesting. Almost without exception, people talk about the man who invested a lifetime in building this shrine. All express admiration for his skill and dedication.

But thoughts about God and a desire to worship Him are conspicuously absent. Many people capture the site on film or at least buy a post card from the souvenir shop. The picture is destined for an attic, where it will gather dust along with other mementos from summer vacations. If the photo is resurrected at all in later years, it will be remembered purely as a novelty.

From the construction of the shrine itself to the constant snapping of camera shutters, man has an insatiable desire to encapsulate God. When God does something great (or at least is reported to have done something great), we erect a monument or build a building or preserve the original site. Then later we gape, gawk, and burn through rolls of film, as well as buy up a wide variety of souvenirs, to commemorate in some way that *we* have been where *He* has been.

But the shrines, the cathedrals, the color slides, and the home movies all breed gods that are far too small. The attempts to bottle and contain God in buildings, statues, or photographs betray how shabby our thoughts of God can be. Eugene Peterson wrote that the church has been captured by a tourist mind-set.[1] He is right. Nowhere is this more evident than in our worship.

Too many of our services are parched counterfeits—sterile pantomimes convincing us that we've worshiped while cheating us of the real thing. In David's life, forgiven sin loosened his heart and tongue in joyful praise. This response to God is always in season, always appropriate. Worship is a life-changing thing. It certainly is the atmosphere of heaven. Why, then, should we settle for less here and now?

All dried up with nowhere to go

Like twin forks of a dry stream bed, parched counterfeits in the church have at least two expressions. One is *the lifeless assembly*.

A couple of telltale signs characterize the lifeless assembly. One is *visibility without reality*. There is a noticeable lack of depth in the fellowship of many churches. The appearance is there but the reality is missing. Fellowship is more than coffee and donuts, more than getting together with people just like us. It's the unique blending together of people who have one thing in common, that is, that Jesus Christ has saved them and is developing them into people who reflect His image. This common identity in Christ bonds worshipers together and refuses to be silent.

But even church leaders sometimes view those who love conversations on spiritual topics as nuisances, eccentrics, or embarrassments. Our spiritual edges get on each other's nerves. When truth intimidates us and the religious words peppered through our vocabulary become nothing more than buzzwords that the faithful know but fail to understand, worship withers into a bony, emaciated thing. We're all dried up with nowhere to go, spiritually speaking.

Another symptom of a lifeless assembly is *compliance without understanding.* If worship has been devalued in the pew, the cause may be found in the pulpit. If leadership fails to teach people the spiritual nature of the content and rhythm of the worship service, then compliance without understanding is likely to result. What is this? It's going through the motions of singing hymns, reading Scripture, praying, standing up, sitting down, just because the bulletin or order of worship says so. It's a conditioned response to programmed monotony instead of an intentional, enlivened response to God.

P. T. Barnum is alive and well

The entertainment center is the second expression of parched counterfeits. Ringling Brothers has nothing on the spectaculars staged in some churches. Does this mean that God is dishonored or displeased by all large-scale ceremony, liturgy, or presentation? Certainly not. The dedication of Solomon's Temple and the celebration of the rebuilding of Jerusalem's walls under Nehemiah's direction show that God rejoices in large displays of worship. The Bible describes heaven as a realm where worship takes place on an unimaginable scale.

Intentionally focusing on size and spectacle is the issue. When leadership chooses a showboat philosophy of ministry merely to maintain or increase attendance, then motives need examining. When the people in the congregation sit enthralled at our lavish stage productions and leave bedazzled but not deepened in their adoration of God, something is wrong. When talk turns with the final cymbal crash to who's going after the car and where we're going for pie and coffee, we have probably not worshiped.

On the other hand, I once attended a seminar where the speaker brought the crowd, largely pastors, to their feet in praise to God. At the conclusion, my neighbor said he was canceling his lunch plans to be alone with God. Many others did the same. Fellowship could wait. So could crowded restaurants and coffee shops. God had broken out in our midst and we were melted in submission and silence before Him, and attracted to live ever more intimately in His presence.

What is it like to be in the presence of God? Although language pales here, it means basically to feel dwarfed by but strangely drawn to the presence of One far greater than our minds can conceive. Scripture helps with some vivid pictures from the perspectives of Isaiah and John:

> In the year of King Uzziah's death, I saw the Lord sitting on a throne, lofty and exalted, with the train of His robe filling the temple. Seraphim stood above Him, each having six wings; with two he covered his face, and with two he covered his feet, and with two he flew. And one called out to another and said, "Holy, Holy, Holy, is the LORD of hosts, the whole earth is full of His glory." And the foundations of the thresholds trembled at the voice of Him who called out, while the temple was filling with smoke. Then I said, "Woe is me, for I am ruined! Because I am a man of unclean lips . . . for my eyes have seen the King, the LORD of hosts." (Isaiah 6:1-5)

> I turned to see . . . one like a son of man, clothed in a robe reaching to the feet, and girded across His breasts with a golden girdle. And His head and His hair were white like

white wool, like snow; and His eyes were like a flame of fire; and His feet were like burnished bronze, when it has been caused to glow in a furnace, and His voice was like the sound of many waters. And in His right hand He held seven stars; and out of His mouth came a sharp two-edged sword; and His face was like the sun shining in its strength. And when I saw Him, I fell at His feet as a dead man. (Revelation 1:12-17)

There is no hint of a tourist mind-set here. Isaiah doesn't pull out an Instamatic and say, "Wow! I've just got to get a shot of this for Irma and the kids. They'll never believe it!" Although anyone having this experience would be severely shaken, Isaiah seemed to have no desire to flee. This rings true. In genuine worship, we find ourselves drawn to the Lord and hating to leave. Time ceases to matter. Words seem unnecessary, even irreverent. The silence of wonder alone seems fitting. And if silence is broken at all, only words of praise are appropriate.

Unfortunately, we often cheapen praise to the level of a spiritual gratuity. God will get it when He does something to deserve it. David labeled this kind of attitude as a heart still in "bloodguiltiness," in sin. How do we break free of the habit of merely "tipping" God with our church attendance, occasional giving, and sporadic praise? To do so, we must make friends with three attitudes toward God that our culture is geared to resist:

(1) *Majesty* is reverent respect due the splendor of royalty. American culture knows little of it. We no longer respect authority figures as we once did. Besides, loyalty to a king is foreign, even repulsive to us. The average man's idea of democracy is a place "where I can do anything I want." This definition tips our hand. It shows we have a deep-seated, self-centered reinforcement against our appreciation of God's majesty.

(2) *Awe* means being struck speechless with wonder. Living in a world overgrown with jaded cynicism and calloused sensitivi-

ties, we are getting progressively tougher to shock, stun, surprise, move, or impress. We're sophisticated and "laid back." Television and radio help to inure us by making reality readily available without impact or urgency. It's nothing to sit calmly munching Fritos while the evening news runs a story of five people shot in the streets of Tel Aviv. We would hardly sit munching so calmly were the same five people shot dead in the street in front of our house. Joys and tragedies can thus become a ho-hum affair controlled by a remote-control button.

Another cultural factor cheating us of awe is the fast-paced, transient lifestyle that characterizes much of society. Awe rarely explodes upon us with the poof of a flash bulb. More often than not it must wash over us and soak in to be fully realized, and that takes time—something our frantic days just have too little of. In getting from here to there we ignore galaxies, sunsets, violets, and veins on a leaf. Contemplation and meditation are two skills that cannot be improved with a home computer. Awe is an elusive thing for those who run rapid-fire through their days.

(3) Unlike majesty and awe, *fear* is very much with us. But in contrast to the kind of fear we should have in worship, our usual fear is often a selfish thing, a knee-jerk response when the security of our self-interest is threatened in any way. In contrast, fear in worship is an unnerving experience that makes mere respect pale by comparison. It means standing with Isaiah, and saying, "I am undone."

The episode of Jesus' calming of the storm (Mark 4:36-41) is a perfect example of the contrast between human fear and the fear of God. Jesus was asleep in the boat as He and the Twelve crossed the Sea of Galilee. A sudden storm arose. Swells washed into the boat, and even the experienced sailors among them were afraid. Responding to their plea for help with a mild rebuke, Jesus calmed the wind and waves. Before He spoke, fear of death gripped the men. But after Jesus spoke and they felt the wind die and the boat stop bucking, they were even more afraid. Not many recognize this unusual note. What kind of fear could be greater than a fear of death? The fear of the Author of life! When was the last time God absolutely astonished you with His sheer power, when you no longer felt like staying within the safe, controllable confines of your agenda but felt compelled to huddle humbly at His feet?

Men have an inbred hunger to know God and see His greatness. Even though our more direct, personal glimpses of Him may be few, our response to Him should always be spontaneous and instinctive. David's praise flowed freely. That's the way it should be with all of us. The church does not have to wait to sample the exalting chorus of heaven. Rather, we must be willing to be transformed from lifeless assemblies and entertainment centers to the people of God, people who delight in praising the sublime, majestic Author of life. He simply refuses to be imprisoned either in color slides or in a one-hour time slot on Sundays. Rather, He wants our undivided attention, our entire being. When His people gather, He alone is the audience—an audience of One.

NOTES:

1. Eugene Peterson, *A Long Obedience in the Same Direction* (Downers Grove, Illinois: InterVarsity Press, 1980), page 12.

CHAPTER TWELVE

Living with a Broken Heart

O Lord, open my lips,
That my mouth may declare Thy praise.
For Thou dost not delight in sacrifice, otherwise I would give it;
Thou art not pleased with burnt offering.
The sacrifices of God are a broken spirit;
A broken and a contrite heart, O God, Thou wilt not despise.
Psalm 51:15-17

■

The winter of 1944 clutched Europe in its iciest grip in decades. Fresh wounds of war froze into jagged scars across northern France as Allied and German forces were bogged down in the ice, snow, and mud, staring at one another like exhausted boxers in opposing corners.

The Allies gambled that the Germans would dig in and wait until spring to counterattack. They were wrong. Unknown to air surveillance, massive reinforcements of battle-hardened troops assembled behind German lines. In a movement Hitler himself designed to reverse the Allied offensive, leading to what would be called the Battle of the Bulge, the Germans roared out of the snow-swirled darkness into the faces of the greenest American troops in Europe. The situation was grim. Casualties were high. Units were disorganized and the Nazi onslaught was ruthless.

Although many fought and died, the presence of one man made the difference. Stripped of an earlier command, the man chafed and grumbled at a desk in England. But desperate times seem tailored for unorthodox men. He was called to France, and indeed this decision proved to be pivotal to the situation evolving in Europe. As frightened men lay freezing in foxholes, the sight of this intrepid leader waving and yelling from his jeep as it careened around shell holes brought renewed strength and courage to those troops. He personified the fire and commitment needed to reverse the Nazi breakout. This valiant, eccentric man was General George S. Patton. Those American soldiers suffering the agonies of freezing weather and exploding shells didn't need lectures on courage. They needed to see someone who really had it.

Seeing is understanding

Abstract ideas, philosophies, and qualities such as courage are often so slippery and elusive that only a few can grasp them. But when these ideas take on flesh, the resulting impact can span oceans, decades, and centuries, and affect millions of people. The lives of Moses, Plato, Mohammed, Buddha, Marx, Hitler, and Gandhi serve as examples. But nowhere has this kind of impact been more evident than in the life of Jesus Christ. The pinnacle of the revelation of God wasn't leaked through a press agent drooling hype into a bouquet of microphones at the Holiday Inn. John said that "the Word became flesh, and dwelt among us, and we beheld His glory, glory as of the only begotten from the Father, full of grace and truth" (John 1:14).

Sadly, although we believe in doctrines such as the Incarnation and the virgin birth, we lose too easily a sense of wonder and awe that they could have happened in the first place. There were few theologians at the cradle in Bethlehem. The Incarnation event was something common shepherds, sweaty fishermen, adulterous women, ostracized lepers, the crippled, the blind, and the demon crazed were ripe and gratified to sink their teeth into. They saw the Reality of that doctrine up-close. If God had remained aloof from fallen men, those of us in the trenches would be left to grope our way through life, and God would be nothing more than an intellectual toy. But Paul, John, Peter, and others had such a powerful effect through the course of history not because they had invented or inherited a message, but because they had encountered one.

> What was from the beginning, what we have heard, what we have seen with our eyes, what we beheld and our hands handled, concerning the Word of life—and the life was manifested, and we have seen and bear witness and proclaim to you the eternal life, which was with the Father and was manifested to us—what we have seen and heard we proclaim to you also. . . . (1 John 1:1-3)

Where rubber meets the road

The laboratory of Christianity is the breeding ground of life. It's here that the fruit of the Spirit sprouts like seeds and Christ's nature is hammered out in our personalities. Paul's statement that we are to be conformed to the image of Jesus Christ isn't just sanctified rhetoric but a statement that points us toward realities we have yet to dream of and embrace.

In an age of many different approaches to spirituality, the acid test for many people is practicality. Simply, does it work? Can an idea stand the strain of the marketplace where men feel pain, endure frustration, and finally die? Jesus Christ demonstrated to His followers that these hard-to-accept teachings were workable through the way He lived.

Although we don't know Christ up-close and face-to-face, we still need living examples of His grace and righteousness. The Church of the Prematurely Enfeebled grows rapidly, filling its ranks with those who have great promise but who wallow in mediocrity. They view the life described in the New Testament as a distant, unreachable ideal.

Sometimes I need to see the Spirit working through someone

around me—just to remind myself that His Reality is our reality, too. My life often seems like a construction site where the work has been started but the crew has been on a long break. So I wonder when the work is going to continue. The effect of just one person showing the evidence of God's presence can't be over-stated. When someone who is in love with God crosses the path of disillusioned, lukewarm Christians, that person can strategically strike a spark of hope and confidence that may well make the difference between them following Christ or pulling aside into some stagnant backwater.

Almost everyone can think of a living example of godliness. A retired missionary running a bookstore, a businessman, and a college roommate all showed Christ in their lives in ways that molded me. Just reflecting back on their lives brings strength and encouragement to me.

Not far from my home is what is billed as the world's largest carousel. Over three stories high, it is a whirling spectacle of over 10,000 lights and 300 animals (no two alike and no horses!). People gawk at it and snap pictures. But while the carousel draws large crowds, no one has ever ridden it!

What makes people draw near the church for a closer look, only to have them wander away without ever getting into the saddle? David told us the answer when he described certain sacrifices and burnt offerings that God would not accept. But why wouldn't God accept them? Because He looks on the heart. God is never satisfied with externals alone. Tossing a few pineapples or a beautiful maiden into a volcano may satisfy the gods of the South Seas in a grade-B movie. But the real God demands that a man's life and heart stand plumb with his worship, not contrary to it. That's why the swirling carousel of visible religion often attracts lost men and women but cannot hold them for long unless all they want is a feeding ground for their own pride.

When sincere people get close to some of our churches that resemble a carnival sideshow, they can sense in short order that we are imitating a world that has already left them weary and wanting more. Not many people are willing to ride our evangelical carousels anymore. More and more of our critics are speaking up. Maybe the unpleasant aroma of our offerings is driving them away.

An unfulfilled cry rings out from the famished faith of many people. Adults share it with me over club sandwiches, and the youth throw it at me with their eyes on Sunday. They both ask, "It can't really be as good as you say, can it?" While I rush to give reassurances, they can only seem to remember the weak-kneed caricature of faith they've seen all their lives.

Who can these people look to? Pastors up on a pedestal at such a lofty altitude where no flaws are visible offer little encouragement. Fears of failure and of being unmasked keep many pastors hiding behind the office instead of rejoicing openly in the call. And what about parents who are coping poorly with guilt over their past mistakes and inconsistent lifestyles? They already feel pressured by rebellious adolescents, lack of free time, and society's expectations.

Who, then, is adequate for the role of being an example of the unconditional love of Christ? Not many. That's precisely why we should be compassionate with skeptics. Many of them were some of the keenest seekers after God, but their hopes and dreams just couldn't outdistance their disillusionment. They never saw the rubber really meet the road. That's why laymen, youth, and skeptics need the same thing we all need to bolster our determination to follow Christ: the signpost of an authentic Christian life instead of empty sacrifices.

While General Patton may not be the prototype of this life, David portrayed it admirably. The broken spirit and contrite heart always please God. Remember Jacob and his disjointed thigh? A person dwelling deeply with God will include brokenness among his fondest treasures and ablest mentors. The sheer arrogance so easily passed off as boldness today is repulsive. The church needs

followers of Christ who limp—at least in heart if not the thigh—
because they daily pass through the flurry of the spiritual battle.

Two jewels worth finding

What is this brokenness? Having a broken, contrite heart means
seeing our own sin as blacker than anyone else's. That's how, in
our attitudes, we can become more gracious to others who may be
aggravating or unlovable. In daily life, we must decide not to
indulge the tantrums and clamoring of our flesh. This heart-
wounding of brokenness is almost always painful. But we need to
willingly endure it in order to nurture certain capacities in our
lives—two jewels in particular that are well worth finding.

One of those capacities is *teachability*. A truly broken person
is convinced that God has something worthwhile to say to him,
and that he will hear Him out even if values, attitudes, and lifestyle
must change. He never feels that he knows so much about living
the Christian life that God's counsel is irrelevant. Knowledge of
even a little spiritual truth can be intoxicating.

The subversive way our pride delights in what *we* know
instead of what God knows is paralyzing to the way we live.
Rigidity and judgmental attitudes quickly set in, killing off growth.
But a teachable person knows something of brokenness. His
capacity for growth is unlimited.

The capacity for *genuine spiritual leadership* also roots best
in a broken life. Almost all groups have two types of leadership:
positional and real. Positional leadership has the title and the name
on the door. Real leadership actually shapes opinion and direction. Spiritual leadership is never purely positional. An anointing
of God can never be assumed on the basis of a Formica name plate
or a majority vote.

In Shakespeare's *Julius Caesar*, Caesar described Cassius as
a man with "a lean and hungry look." Ambition caused his jaws to
be slack and drooling. While Scripture encourages those who are
aspiring to leadership (1 Corinthians 12:31, 1 Timothy 3:1), it also

warns that only God's initiative, choosing, and timing can make a spiritual leader (1 Peter 5:6). A broken man or woman will wait.

Scripture encourages us with several models. But the way we unduly exalt spiritual leaders does us in. Lives from the Bible that were meant to help us often only intimidate us. We don't see much of ourselves in people like Paul. But we should. They were people who, in spite of their flaws and failings, saw the life of Jesus Christ fleshed out in their daily lives. Let's consider Paul for a moment. In an age without overhead projectors, blackboards, and flannel-graphs, the primary visual aid Paul used to illustrate his teaching was his own life.

> Be imitators of me, just as I also am of Christ. (1 Corinthians 11:1)

> Brethren, join in following my example, and observe those who walk according to the pattern you have in us. (Philippians 3:17)

Although Paul's life was far from sinless, we should be encouraged that his life was still considered worthy of imitation. Every Christian should take heart that if the Holy Spirit was able to show Jesus Christ through the personality of the cantankerous, iron-willed apostle Paul, then not one of us is too difficult a case for Him. The preceding verses should make us think carefully when we realize that people within our sphere of influence will be to some degree conformed to our image as well as to Christ's. It happens. We can see it in our kids. Many parents painfully learn that their adolescent children do not turn out exactly as they may have desired. Instead, these young people embody both positive and negative aspects of the family value structure.

In spiritual leadership, things work out the same way. How often have pastors and other leaders complained about the attitudes of those in their care? Charges of bitterness, resentment, detachment, spiritual blindness, and lack of commitment are common. Is it possible that in many cases, churches tend to merely echo attitudes and behavior that is being modeled by the unrelenting pressure, personal disappointments, unfulfilled hopes, and unrealistic expectations of their leaders? The leaders project these negative attitudes onto the people, who, consciously or otherwise, reciprocate. Often the institutional and spiritual crises that leaders face are simply evidence of our inability to cope with spiritual Frankensteins of our own making.

Each one of us can have the kind of broken and contrite heart that makes God smile and makes other people follow. But first we must field a relevant and very personal question. Do we genuinely want all the things we pray for, things such as more spiritual power, wider usefulness, and God's glory? The trivialities that can so easily repel us embarrassingly remind us that "the kingdom of God does not consist in words, but in power" (1 Corinthians 4:20).

Talk is cheap. Many of our lives resemble littered highways strewn with wadded-up promises and crushed, rusting intentions. We daydream about the heights and do nothing more than pout over our refusal to climb them. Mere lip service to the Cross of Christ must be shaken off, freeing us to embrace the low and difficult things of life. Our sweet tooth for blessings needs to be curtailed, while an appetite to share in the growth process of suffering (Romans 8:17-18), humility (2 Corinthians 4:7-11), weakness (2 Corinthians 12:7-10), and discipline (Hebrews 12:4-11) needs to be cultivated.

Is this intense kind of life really for us? If something deep inside you warms to the idea of being taught by God in both the valleys and the peaks, then the kernel of an obedient life is already sprouting. The richness of an abundant life can be not only for you; it can also be for those who observe the exciting adventure of your life. A few pointed questions will gauge how serious we really are.

Test yourself

Can you ask forgiveness? After all, if Jesus is Lord, then it's only important for *Him* to be right all the time. How many times have churches been wounded and friendships destroyed because someone just couldn't choke out the words "I'm sorry"? Confessing sin to God is hard at times. But in a very real way, it's sometimes harder to confess our sin to another person. Strangely enough, one of the most spiritual things someone can say is "I was wrong. I'm sorry." Can you do it?

Can you forgive freely? As difficult as asking forgiveness can be, granting it can be just as tough. Pride knows no rest on either side of a wrong. Forgiving means absorbing the pain of the wrong for the sake of restoring the relationship with the offender. In other cases, it means we forgive as Christians because God forgave us. And it's done without gloating or resentment. Paul said, "Be kind to one another, tender-hearted, forgiving each other, just as God in Christ also has forgiven you" (Ephesians 4:32).

Is restoring relations with another Christian and maintaining the unity of God's church more important than being vindicated or getting what we perceive as our rights? Of course. We shouldn't do things for God because it's easy or to our advantage. We should do them because we're in tune with His will. Forgiveness is one of the clearest indications that we understand God's dealings with us.

Are you free to fail? Our growth in Christ will speed up when we realize that God has never committed Himself to concealing our weaknesses and mistakes. In fact, God absolutely refused to hide the lusts of David, the connivings of Jacob, the unbelief of Abraham, and the inconsistency of Peter. God's Word tells the good, the bad, and the ugly.

Phrases such as "I don't know" or "I was wrong" have become a Christian obscenity for many. But why? Admitting a mistake has never shattered genuine Christianity or real leadership. When does anyone's faith stand or fall on a pretense of perfection? In all honesty, given the Fall, all Christians function at various levels of error, incompetence, and sin. Any posturing about being better than others is not only unbecoming, but it is distasteful and dishonest. When we slyly try to wear God's attributes as if they were our own, we look like a little boy slogging around in his father's clothes. Well-tailored words like omniscience fit God sharply and snugly, but look rumpled and droopy on us. The fear of failure has a fierce grip on many people. This should be a warning to us that it might not be God's Kingdom we're building. We need to take a good look at our motives.

Can you admit need? It's sad to see the hobbling disillusionment fledgling Christians encounter when they discover that their new faith isn't trial-free or temptation-proof. The image of a problem-free Christian life, bathed in continuous "Praise the Lords," is a lie. Can it really be true that growing older in both grace and years is marked by an absence of need? Or is it only our pride clutching frantically for some fig leaves to conceal the fact that passing years haven't been accompanied by deepening grace?

Contrast this with Paul. A striking little nugget lies in 2 Corinthians 7:5-6. Writing about his entry into Macedonia, Paul described the beautiful irony of God's grace in the midst of our adversity.

> Even when we came into Macedonia our flesh had no rest, but we were afflicted on every side: conflicts without, fears within. But God, who comforts the depressed, comforted us by the coming of Titus. (2 Corinthians 7:5-6)

Paul had needs. So do we. Perhaps the greatest contribution mature Christians can make is to discreetly but honestly share their current needs and struggles. Too often our fearful silence is mistaken for strength.

Are you free from the need to be justified in the eyes of others? This spiritual foible is so subtle! Who hasn't been unjustly accused or misunderstood? When it happens, the urge to set things right is strong. When we're misunderstood, the yearning for approval and the good opinion of others runs deep.

In those weak moments when the longing to set things right and make everyone understand smolders within, 1 Peter 2:20 supplies solid support: "What credit is there if, when you sin and are harshly treated, you endure it with patience? But if when you do what is right and suffer for it you patiently endure it, this finds favor with God."

There are times in everyone's life when what God is doing is impossible to explain. Our actions are misread by even those closest to us, and any attempt to explain only complicates things. At those times, the approval we need most is never found in those furtive glances over our shoulder to see which of our friends, colleagues, and family members are applauding our decisions and commitments. Only the most misunderstood and rejected One in history knows how we feel, and it's His "well done" alone that is needed.

Will someone be inspired to excellence for Christ because of your life? A broken and contrite heart is a formidable thing in God's hand. His Kingdom advances on the shoulders of those who refuse to be put off or satisfied with less. And I, for one, long to be among them. Paul said it so well:

> We have this treasure in earthen vessels, that the surpassing greatness of the power may be of God and not from our-selves; we are afflicted in every way, but not crushed; per-plexed, but not despairing; persecuted, but not forsaken; struck down, but not destroyed; always carrying about in the body the dying of Jesus, that the life of Jesus also may be manifested in our body. (2 Corinthians 4:7-10)

I recently received a letter from an old friend. Bob's life showed me Jesus Christ in a way that made me want Him even more for myself. Was Bob a "super-Christian"? No, far from it.

But he allowed me the privilege of seeing his life as it was.

Interpersonal conflict sanded Bob's rough edges smooth. A relationship with a girl he intended to marry was broken off. Because it conflicted with his love for Christ, he gave up a sport he loved. For Bob, becoming humble involved a broken ankle, which made him dependent on others for almost everything. He endured many rebukes from others. And on one memorable night, I saw him face his sin squarely, when he could have covered it by trying to save face in front of me. But no fig leaves for Bob. He refused himself the luxury of them for Christ's sake—and for mine.

In all these situations, I never saw Bob chafe. In the letter I recently received from Bob, he shared that a gentler side of his nature has come out in the past few years. The roots of that gentleness wind all the way back to the basement room we shared at college. In the years since then, I have had experiences quite parallel to those Bob persevered through. Although some of them hurt deeply, I grew through them. Because of what I'd seen in Bob's life, I could trust God to use discouragement, rebuke, heartbreak, and failure to hammer my stubborn will into His image.

Broken and contrite hearts are rare. But God loves them. They are the basic raw material through which He works. God treasures every man and woman who lives boldly with a broken heart—*truly* lives. This kind of life is such a rare prize that it is recognized by everyone who observes it. Whether a life is broken over sin, pain, persecution, or service to the Master, people see it shine so rarely that they want that depth of character for themselves in place of the shabby idols of this world. Many people are so moved by the strength and wisdom that comes out of brokenness that they are willing to take another look at the God who repairs a broken heart.

The time is ripe, in fact compelling, for the rare exception to the common, shabby rule. It takes a willingness to go against the grain, sometimes even the ecclesiastical grain. But Jesus went against that same kind of opposition. Lives where He fits like a hand in a glove, where He diffuses like an excellent perfume, are the stuff that can give a new birth of hope to others who can receive His life as their own.

CHAPTER THIRTEEN

Seeking the Firefall

By Thy favor do good to Zion;
Build the walls of Jerusalem.
Then Thou wilt delight in righteous sacrifices,
In burnt offering and whole burnt offering;
Then young bulls will be offered on Thine altar.
Psalm 51:18-19

■

The Outer Hebrides Islands possess a rugged beauty. Isolated, rainy, and cold, these dark green jewels sprinkled across the North Atlantic off the coast of Scotland spawn and sustain a hearty people. Living there isn't easy, but heart roots are sunk deep into the rocky soil, so visitors hear no complaints. Eyes crinkled from warm smiles and from staring down winter winds testify that here man and nature have settled into the roles of two old adversaries who have begrudgingly won each other's respect.

One of the smallest of these islands, Berna, is home for five hundred inhabitants. Reachable only by ferry, the place is one of those obscure corners of the globe. In comparison with New York or London, it might seem insignificant. Besides the residents, who would care what went on there? God did. He broke in on them so powerfully that lives were changed overnight in what can be described by only one word: *revival.*

The postmaster, Hector MacKinnon, had long been seized

145

with deep anguish and sorrow over the spiritually empty lives surrounding him. Driven to the solitude of his barn by this passion, he spent a day on his face praying for the people of Berna. In response, God brought a noted preacher, Duncan Campbell, to the island for a service. A mingling of habitual attenders and curiosity seekers straggled into the rickety white church overlooking the sea.

Campbell preached. Nothing happened. Unable to hide his bewilderment, Campbell stood on the front steps watching the people wind their way down the grassy slope. Appearing at his elbow, MacKinnon said, "I hope you're not disappointed that revival did not come to the church tonight. But God is hovering over us and will break through any minute."

Even as he spoke, the sea breezes that constantly swirled around the hill eased to a whisper and then stopped. Suddenly the people ambling down the hill knelt and wept in the heather. The power of God seized the island. Many in town who had not attended the earlier service were now strangely possessed with a sense of sin. Almost every home was touched. The glory of God became public domain and concern.

Fire from heaven

What constitutes spiritual awakening or revival? Much of today's swirl of activities seems strangely out of place. Fueled by frantic activity and multicolored brochures, churches often want God to move in ways that add bodies to the membership rolls but can be controlled by a majority vote of a business meeting or a committee. In this parody of real awakening, we are guilty of aping some unsavory predecessors.

Many years ago on Mt. Hermon, the priests of Baal stood blood-smeared and exhausted. Leering and swaggering a few hours earlier, they did everything they knew to bring their god down, but failed. It wasn't so much the shocked looks of disbelief on the faces of the crowd that hurt. It was the humiliating taunts of one man standing alone against them that stung like a swarm of bees.

Rough as an old cob, Elijah was a man who still reaches out from the page and grabs the reader by the collar. That day, he stood infuriated at these drooping, bloody religious professionals who had led the people around by their lusts for years. Elijah knew how men tend to flock to anything that makes their hedonistic desires look respectable and religious.

But now it was time to reveal if Elijah's "god" was also a fraud. The wood of Elijah's sacrifice was stacked and soaked with water. Standing beside the dripping logs, Elijah lifted his eyes and prayed. At that moment fire fell from heaven (1 Kings 18:38). Rocks, wood, and water sizzled as the flames licked them up like candy. Elijah's god was *God.* One prayer from that God did it. This was a prayer that had simmered to a boiling point in the cauldron that had become Elijah's heart.

Hector MacKinnon, that postmaster in little Berna, had this heart, this intensity. But our lives are often too easily nibbled away to possess it for long, if at all. We're consumed from a number of directions like numerous small fires crawling sleepily and smokily over matted grass and leaves. What we need to see is the glory of an unleashed God, the outwardly expanding ripples of divine power that men can neither control nor command. Is media promotion and the whirl of activities surrounding what we popularly call "revival" unnecessary? No. But our preoccupation with these peripheral things, these outward paraphernalia of revival, shows our displaced focus in spite of our theology. Jacques Ellul pins us down when he says, "We still find it hard to believe today that prayer is more important than action."[1]

Christ's church needs awakening. Our efforts have seen too much of the carnival sideshow and not enough of the heart that was poured out on that barn floor on an island in the North Atlantic. Ellul is right: we would rather act out God's work in shallow pantomime. Even though the results are temporary, it is safer. As long as God appears to work through channels we can control, our comfortable status is still quo. We want titillation by the Divine, a tantalizing flirtation with God that lifts our emotions but leaves the sediment of our souls unstirred. We want to remain comfortably numb.

But we *must* have more! We inherently know that. Many are praying for it. But how will we know when real awakening comes? David pointed to the most telling aspect of awakening visible in any age: an alive body of believers penetrating the surrounding society.

From the church to the streets

Spiritual life in Old Testament times was never a private affair. The strength of Israel's relationship with God could be measured by observing the political situation at any given time. When the leaders and the people of Israel honored the covenant that God had established, the nation accordingly prospered and expanded its borders against all enemies. But as idolatry infected the people, who were easily influenced by the example set by their wayward kings, the results were inevitable: moral decay, political corruption, national deline, and spiritual bankruptcy. The benchmarks of creeping coldness weren't necessarily declines in Sunday school and worship attendance. When men like Amos spoke against the situation of their day, they looked to the streets as well as to the Temple:

> They hate him who reproves in the gate, and they abhor
> him who speaks with integrity. Therefore, because you
> impose heavy rent on the poor and exact a tribute of grain
> from them, though you have built houses of well hewn
> stone, yet you will not live in them. . . . I know your trans-
> gressions are many and your sins are great, you who distress
> the righteous and accept bribes, and turn aside the poor in
> the gate. (Amos 5:10-12)

David was justified in asking God's favor for the city of Jerusalem in Psalm 51:18. For many of us, the Temple and the streets are far apart. But men like David, Amos, and others were not nearsighted in their view of redemption. They saw things from the full vista of a cosmic and biblical perspective. To them, God was a Creator working to restore His ravaged creation. Salvation was not merely a personal thing. It had to hit the pavement in a confrontation of sin.

The miracles and teachings of Jesus wind this thread of God's concern into a full tapestry. Not only did He point out the more "blatant" sins that land people in prison. Jesus also stood against prejudice, materialism, and neglect of the poor. Almost every outbreak of revival power in church history has resulted in a penetrated society. Men like John Wesley and Charles Finney waxed as red-hot for social reform as for the salvation of their hearers. Scripture describes a Savior who is not just Lord of the church but of the world.

> He is the image of the invisible God, the first-born of all creation. For in Him all things were created, both in the heavens and on earth, visible and invisible, whether thrones or dominions or rulers or authorities—all things have been created through Him and for Him. And He is before all things, and in Him all things hold together. (Colossians 1:15-17)

Certainly a Savior this large has concerns broader than my personal well-being and that of my local church. If He is truly Lord, then no area of human existence is outside the scope of His concern. Christians should claim areas of secular expertise such as economics, technology, medicine, education, mass media, and politics as part of His domain. Since these fields shape society, we need to engage them from a Christian perspective. Professions in these disciplines can be ministries advancing Christ's Kingdom.

Framing it well, John Wesley said, "Christianity is essentially a social religion; to turn it into a solitary religion is indeed to destroy it."[2]

The fire must start at home

But in wanting to see society changed, we feel some major frustrations nibbling away within us. How can the world be changed when we see so little change in ourselves? By sugar-coating Marxist agendas with Christian language, liberation theologians mistakenly think that the deepest changes happen by changing structures alone. An overthrow of the government or a new constitution cannot straighten out the twists of the human heart.

And whose heart doesn't need some straightening out? David's did. Mine does. How about yours? Earlier in Psalm 51, David spoke about sacrifices God would not accept. Now, in the final verse, he points to the kind of sacrifices God welcomes: righteous ones. Whenever and wherever God's people offer Him gifts of honest confession and repentance, their lives will resonate with perseverance and power.

This is true awakening. This is genuine revival that cuts wide swaths of evangelism and social ministry through the surrounding culture. The fire of revival must start at home. How can a heart fired with love for Christ rest while there are people who don't know Him or people who are being crushed under the oppression of others? History teaches that both of these concerns are honest expressions of the Holy Spirit. Men like Wilberforce and Shaftesbury in nineteenth-century England were products of spiritual awakening and shine as examples of the impact redeemed men can have in society.

> The greatest achievements of the century—the abolition of the slave trade, reform of prisons, emancipation of slaves, care of the sick, education of the young, protection of

workers and the like were made . . . by enlightened individuals . . . nurtured in the faith and worship of evangelical fellowships.[3]

Too many Christians endure an undeserved berating for their weak witness and their failure to get involved in ministry. Their leaders beat them into bottomless despair, leaving pews filled with sincere but paralyzed and discouraged people. Can God's Spirit sweep into our hearts and churches as He did on that windswept hillside in the North Atlantic? Are the movements of the Spirit that are associated with historical awakenings and the book of Acts a thing of the past? Prospects for spiritual awakening often swing on the fragile hinges of attitudes. A few probes will test the mettle of our desires.

A spiritual checkup
We all need a spiritual checkup from time to time. Try this one out for size. The first probe is an examination of your thinking. Has your way of looking at spiritual things become numbed? Does your ego tend to dominate your mind-set? Is your prayer often cosmetic? How much of what you and your church do is really God-dependent? We need to let God guide us in everything. When the Holy Spirit breaks loose, no program defined on flip charts or dictated by a majority vote can contain or restrain Him.

The second probe checks your eyesight. Can you distinguish between what is merely novel and what is truly divine? All of us tend to get bored quickly. Our attention spans have short fuses. Yesterday's marvel leaves us yawning. Pocket calculators, stereo phonographs, color televisions, and other goodies of technology once sent people running to stores. Now we pass them by, quickly running to other toys. The advertisers know just how gullible we can be. Packaging shouts, "New and improved." How could it be otherwise?

Hasn't it occurred to any of us that the new may only be

novel? The fads and trends of the religious marketplace play the
Christian public as if they were a score of violins. Sometimes we
are guilty of more than gullibility. Our lust for the new is sometimes an avoidance of something old, something tried and true.
Many problems and frustrations in living a Christian life stem
from ignoring truth from God that we already know rather than
failing to pursue something we've yet to learn. Mere novelty in
Christianity may be nothing more than the barometer measuring
how far deadness can proliferate.

A third probe examines our activity—not our sincere service
to God but our frantic, habitual, directionless activity. Lots of
people are frothing in the rut. Can we understand commitment in
terms other than more sweat? Surely when God stirs us deeply He
has more to say than "Get busier! Take on another committee
chairmanship."

Scripture says that the prize of knowing God goes to the one
who, among other things, can be tranquil and still. Tragically, our
lives often become disengaged from our faith and we find ourselves too busy trying to serve God to spend time with Him. In our
confusion, we think that God is pleased. But He's not. He still
wants our works to spring from our faith instead of actually
competing with it.

A fourth probe asks whose kingdom we're really building.
"Unless the LORD builds the house, they labor in vain who build
it" (Psalm 127:1). In wanting revival, in wanting righteous sacrifices that God will accept, we must choose. Who will build? The
cry for progressive "egocide" must ring out. We must stop clinging
to the church as an arena where selfishness is rationalized to
accommodate our worldly appetites.

Churches who consider their doctrine to be seemingly airtight contain some of the most bitter, hateful people. They sugar-
coat their selfish, hidden agendas with phony spiritual language,
polluting church business meetings with religious game-playing.
The way blackmail is used to influence decisions (threats to move

memberships, withhold funds, etc.) is a disgrace.

The silent insistence that everyone conform not only to Christ's standards but to our own, as well, hangs mustily in the air of our church services. And just as any visitor is more sensitive than the residents to odors in a home, people can smell a spiritual deadness about us that dwarfs and obscures our doctrine. The way personal life goals, career choices, spending habits, and choices of marriage partners are systematically excluded from God's counsel is frightening. Some repentance is in order before God can be free to do good to Zion. Both in individuals and in churches, we must decide, sometimes painfully, that God alone is worthy to build.

High stakes faith

The stakes are high. Whether a church is large or small, it becomes big-bottomed when members sit stewing in a dead status quo. If God's church were simply an organization, non-involvement might be an option. But the church is the body of Christ, a vibrant spiritual organism. What would happen in our bodies if a heart valve decided to cease functioning or a mass of cells lurched off independently intent on itself? This would not be a sign of health, but a prelude to death.

But in many corners of the church, encouragement is sprouting. Many people have healthy spiritual appetites they just can't shake. A desire to taste something real of God gnaws deeply within. Nothing less will do. But whether you're riding the crest, wallowing in despair, or wondering if the yearnings you feel will ever be met, hope may be nearer than you think. God designs appetites as cavities of authentic human need. Whether it's for food, love, or God, an appetite is the necessary forerunner of the satisfaction of that appetite. The two are in proportion; as is one, so the other needs to be.

It's easy to appease a shallow hunger. A little insignificant munching will do. But a deep hunger can be an inherent guide. The satisfaction found in Christ is as deep as the most persistent, gnawing yearning for God. Scripture gives us a target, a glimpse, and a foretaste of righteousness taking root in human personality. Paul says in Romans 8:29, "Whom He foreknew, He also predestined to become conformed to the image of His Son, that He might be the first-born among many brethren."

Sanctification, the process by which we become like Christ, is a gradual process that both surges and sputters throughout all our lives. Its end lies in eternity. That's not to say that its end is in doubt. It is not. Neither is its design. Our brittle natures will be softened and shaped until they fully resemble the One who delighted to do the Father's will. In the face of doubts and discouragements, the spiritual genes of this process sometimes seem to be lying dormant, as we leadenly suppose that days of grace have passed us by. But Paul and John bring us back to the truth.

> I am confident . . . that He who began a good work in you will perfect it until the day of Christ Jesus. (Philippians 1:6)

> We know that [when He appears] we shall be like Him, because we shall see Him just as He is. (1 John 3:2)

For those who are struggling with this process of spiritual growth, a day is coming when the realities that seemed like tantalizing illusions will lie in our hands. Those rash statements we sometimes make about all the questions we'll have in heaven show that our thinking is askew. The whole concept implies that getting our questions answered will be some kind of major item on heaven's agenda.

But eternity will show that God is so much larger than we ever dreamed and that questions so important to us now will no doubt seem insignificant and even forgotten then. Our brokenness will be fully repaired. Even those who knew Him best will be awestruck with the splendor of our Savior. The humbling experience will be deep, yet strangely warm, as we gaze on the excellence, the infinite wonder of Christ. That One as magnificent as He would address us like an old friend will overwhelm us as an unspeakable privilege.

And while Jesus Christ will be the center of splendor in eternity, another feature of heaven will leave us almost as limp. We'll absolutely marvel at what He has made us to be. The toddling of our fumbling attempts to follow Christ will give way to spiritual legs that take long, sure strides. Tongues that are just freshly weaned from sin will have only praises for the Lamb. Even angels who live in His presence will stand amazed at the utter sublimity of God's new paradise. Soul tapestries that are now frayed and unraveling will glisten like new, embroidered with the crest of the King.

Our view of this future glory slips away all too easily. Those hints and glimpses in Scripture are the magnetic points that keep us looking at "things unseen." F. W. Robertson once wrote, "My experience is closing into this: that I turn with disgust from everything to Christ." Hasn't an addiction to mediocrity strangled the hopes of too many Christians already? Hasn't a shackled church sleepwalked long enough?

Christians should never rest with distant, misty views of eternity. The things the Bible promises are sometimes as close as our feeblest prayer. They are within reach. But we must decide. Will it be the unadorned yet priceless treasures of Jesus Christ or the shimmering baubles our egos drool over, which are comparatively worthless?

My yearning is that God will grip His people with a deep hunger, and that we will stand up with courage to fully possess and *be* what He is making us to be—to dance despite our broken bones, to dance *because* of them. The results of such commitment are predictable. Many will stare. Some will hate. But others will be drawn—compelled by that unexplainable spiritual magnet God uses to draw people to His Son by breathing out His truth through incomplete lives like ours.

NOTES:
1. Jacques Ellul, "The True Radical," *Discipleship Journal* (January-February 1984), pages 31-33.
2. John Wesley, *Works of John Wesley* (1872 Edition, Volume 5), page 296.
3. J. Edwin Orr, *The Light of the Nations* (Grand Rapids: Eerdmans, 1965), page 229.